ONE OF THE CREW, USS *O'BANNON*, WORLD WAR II

By Walter Allen Lee

WITHDRAWN
Art Circle Public Library

ART CIRCLE PUBLIC LIBRARY
154 East First Street
Crossville, TN 38555-4696
1-931-484-6790

© Copyright 2007 Walter Allen Lee.
All rights reserved. No part of this publication may be reproduced, stored in a retrieval system, or transmitted, in any form or by any means, electronic, mechanical, photocopying, recording, or otherwise, without the written prior permission of the author.

Note for Librarians: A cataloguing record for this book is available from Library and Archives Canada at www.collectionscanada.ca/amicus/index-e.html
ISBN 1-4251-0917-9

Printed in Victoria, BC, Canada. Printed on paper with minimum 30% recycled fibre.
Trafford's print shop runs on "green energy" from solar, wind and other environmentally-friendly power sources.

TRAFFORD PUBLISHING

Offices in Canada, USA, Ireland and UK

Book sales for North America and international:
Trafford Publishing, 6E–2333 Government St.,
Victoria, BC V8T 4P4 CANADA
phone 250 383 6864 (toll-free 1 888 232 4444)
fax 250 383 6804; email to orders@trafford.com

Book sales in Europe:
Trafford Publishing (UK) Limited, 9 Park End Street, 2nd Floor
Oxford, UK OX1 1HH UNITED KINGDOM
phone +44 (0)1865 722 113 (local rate 0845 230 9601)
facsimile +44 (0)1865 722 868; info.uk@trafford.com

Order online at:
trafford.com/06-2675

10 9 8 7 6 5 4 3 2

Dedication

To the "Tin Can" sailors of the United States Navy

Table of Contents

CHAPTER 1 1
USS *O'BANNON* 1
    FACTS ABOUT THE USS *O'BANNON* 2
    ADMIRAL WILLIAM F. HALSEY SPEAKS 4

CHAPTER 2 6
HAWAIIAN ISLANDS 6

CHAPTER 3 9
MARSHALL ISLANDS 9

CHAPTER 4 16
SOLOMON ISLANDS 16

CHAPTER 5 19
NEW GUINEA 19

CHAPTER 6 28
NEW CALEDONIA—AND BACK TO THE SOLOMON ISLANDS 28

CHAPTER 7 37
ADMIRALTY ISLANDS, OR MANUS, ... 37
PAPUA NEW GUINEA 37

CHAPTER 8 40

SOLOMON ISLANDS 40

CHAPTER 9 45
ESPIRITU SANTO, VANUATU, AND GUADALCANAL 45

CHAPTER 10 48
SOLOMON ISLANDS, DUTCH EAST INDIES 48
AND NEW GUINEA 48

CHAPTER 11 66
THE PHILIPPINE ISLANDS 66

CHAPTER 12 163
JAPAN 163

CHAPTER 13 180
HOME!!! 180

CHAPTER 14 181
QUICK OVERVIEW OF PRIOR SERVICE 181
    USS *Pokomoke* 182
    USS *William D. Porter* 184

EPILOGUE 186
A Little Background of My Life Before the US Navy 186

PHOTOGRAPHS 189

GLOSSARY 223

MISCELLANEOUS 231

HAPPY HOUR 231
    Program 231
    CHRONICLES OF *O'BANNON* 234

Preface

This is not intended to be a history book or a treatise on the historical aspects of World War II. I do not discuss strategies or tactics as an officer might; I merely recount the entries in my diary as an enlisted man. I thought it might be interesting to the crew members and their descendants to be able to "see" some of the war through the eyes of a crew member. In my diary, I don't "dress it up" like the media did and does; I just tell it like it is. I'm sure it's not "politically correct."

Although my Navy career encompassed about six years, I have limited the scope of this book to my final ship, the destroyer USS *O'Bannon*. It covers the period from my going aboard the *O'Bannon* and heading out to Pearl Harbor to the signing of the Japanese surrender in Tokyo Bay on 2 September 1945, a period of about one and one-half years.

I was a Radioman 2/C (Second Class), serving in the Communications ("C") Division.

Sometimes I include my own personal feelings, but mostly, I just tell what is going on and where we are. I have omitted some of the boring and hum-drum entries. Also, some of the gripes about my fellow servicemen. As you can imagine, being cooped up with men from all different backgrounds can get fairly touchy at times. I might be bad-mouthing someone one day and praising his heroics the next.

Comments added in parentheses were written by me during 2006, as I prepared this for publication. Comments in brackets were written at the time of the diary entry.

Military time is a 24-hour clock. Four o'clock in the morning is 0400 or 0400 hours; one o'clock p.m. is 1300; eleven o'clock p.m. is 2300, etc.

The Hawaiian Islands were not the 50th state of the United States at the time of World War II; they were a territory of the United States. Also, many other geographical locations may have changed their political status or their name since World War II. I have appended a "Geography" to assist in locating places that I mention. In some cases, I have indicated the various names that they have been called.

You may find that the Chapters are not strictly limited by the locations in the heading. As a destroyer division, we were constantly on the move. The headings are just sort of an indication as to our progression.

I have also appended a Glossary in the event that someone who is not familiar with my terms should read this book.

Also, I have marked a few references in the Index, but those people, ships or places may be referred to many other times in the book. Plus, many people, ships and places may not be in the Index.

Although I did not realize it, these were some of the most significant times of my life. It has taken me many years to be able to discuss these events. I hope that my story may be helpful to someone looking for insight into the feelings of men engaged in a war not of their making.

Please feel free to contact me with your comments and/or corrections. My e-mail address is: totlee@webtv.net, and my mailing address is: Walter Lee, P. O. Box 1828, Fairfield Glade, TN 38558.

                                              Walter A. Lee
                                              Fairfield Glade, Tennessee
                                              15 December 2006

The Second Cruise of the USS *O'Bannon*

1944

18 March	New Guinea Landing Operations[1]
29 May	Shelled Medina Plantation, New Ireland
16-24 October	Reinforce convoy
7-10 December	Landing, Ormoc Bay, the Philippine Islands
15 December	Landing Mindoro, Philippines
26-29 December	Cover Mindoro, Reinforcement echelon

1945

1 January	Landing Lingayen Gulf, Philippine Islands
1 February	Sinking/share RO-115 (a Japanese submarine), 125 nm SW Manila (13-20N, 119-20E)
14-17 February	Corregidor Landing
17 February	Bombarded Ternate Area, south of Manila Bay
24-28 February	Palawan Landing
10 March	Zamboanga Landing
26 March	Cebu Landing

---

[1] A "Landing" is when we go in and bombard Jap positions prior to landing troops.

Second Cruise

27 April	Tarakan, Borneo Landing
1 July-27 August	Raid Ho Islands of Japan
23-29 August	Screen for USS *Missouri*
27 August	Escort for USS *Missouri* into Tokyo Bay
1 September	Tokyo Bay
2 September[2]	Witness Japanese Surrender in Tokyo Bay (some *O'Bannon* crew members aboard the USS *Missouri*). Sail for USA at 1700 hours.

---

[2] Due to the USA being on one side of the International Date Line and Tokyo Bay being on the other, you will see the date of surrender as either 1 September (in Japan) or 2 September (in the USA).

ONE OF THE CREW, USS *O'BANNON*, WORLD WAR II

by Walter Allen Lee

CHAPTER 1

USS *O'BANNON*

This book is an account of my World War II experiences taken from my diaries. My first segment of my USS *O'Bannon* experience begins 3 February 1944. I had been in the Navy since 26 September 1939, and my previous ship was the USS *William D. Porter*, DD579. We had completed the Aleutian Island landings at Adak and Attu. The *William D. Porter* was sunk at Okinawa by a Japanese Kamikaze pilot on 10 June 1945.

I was with the *O'Bannon* right up until we escorted the *Missouri* for the Unconditional Surrender of Japan on 1 September 1945. It was my privilege to be on board the *Missouri* for that historic occasion!

Some records indicate that the *O'Bannon* left the area prior to the surrender being signed—that is not true—I know because I was there.

Some records indicate the surrender was signed on 1 September 1945 and others say 2 September. In trying to figure out why some records are inaccurate, I may have come up with a possible reason. It might be because of the International Date Line. Japan is one day (date) different from the United States. The date in the Eastern hemisphere, to the left of the line, is always one day ahead of the date in the Western hemisphere. The "line" is usually considered to be $180°$ away from the meridian through Greenwich, England.

One of the Crew, *USS O'Bannon*, World War II

FACTS ABOUT THE USS *O'BANNON*

The USS *O'Bannon*, DD 450, that I served on was the second United States Navy ship to be named the *O'Bannon*. Her nickname was "Lucky O" because of her skill or luck in avoiding disaster during the battles of World War II. While I was aboard, she earned twelve battle stars.

The ship was named after Marine Lieutenant Presley Neville O'Bannon, who became known as "the hero of Derna" because of his courage and tenacity in solving a problem with "the Barbary Pirates" in 1805 in Tripoli (now Libya). He was responsible for the Stars and Stripes first being raised on foreign soil. His exploits are memorialized in the Marine Hymn, which contains the words, "From the halls of Montezuma to the shores of Tripoli." O'Bannon was born in 1776, in Virginia, and died 1850, in Kentucky.

The second *O'Bannon* was a Fletcher-class destroyer, built at the Bath Iron Works in Bath, Maine. She was launched 14 March 1942, and commissioned 26 June 1942. She was decommissioned 21 May 1946, but recommissioned 19 February 1951. Her final decommissioning was 30 January 1970, and she was later sold for scrap.

An interesting side-note: The USS *Nicholas*, about which I have written a great deal in my diary, was laid down the same day as the *O'Bannon*, launched the same day as the *O'Bannon*, and commissioned the same day as the *O'Bannon*. We shared many experiences out in the Pacific, and we were truly "sister ships."

The *O'Bannon* was a 2100-ton displacement destroyer, carrying a complement of 329. She had ten torpedo tubes, five 5-inch guns, two 40mm and several 20mm guns, plus depth charges. The Fletcher-class destroyers were the first to be built with radar included. At the time it was built, the *O'Bannon* and other Fletcher-class destroyers were the largest destroyers ever built. Her length was 376.4 feet and her beam was 39.6 feet. Top speed was 38 knots.

During her World War II career, she received the Presidential Unit Citation and seventeen battle stars, more than any other destroyer in the war.

The twelve battle stars the *O'Bannon* earned while I was aboard:

- Consolidation of Solomon Islands: 15 Jun 1944; 22 Jun—24 Aug 1944
- Hollandia Operation (Aitape, Humboldt Bay, Tanahmerah Bay): 21 Apr — 1 May 1944
- Anti-submarine operation: 22 May — 15 June 1944
- Western New Guinea (Morotai Landings): 15 Sep 1944
- Leyte Operation: Leyte Landings 18-29 Oct 1944; Ormoc Bay Landings 7-8 Dec 1944
- Luzon Operation: Mindoro Landings 12-18 Dec 1944; Lingayen Gulf Landings 4-18 Jan 1945
- Anti-submarine assessment-Pacific: 31 Jan 1945
- Consolidation of the Southern Philippine Islands: Palawan Island Landings 28 Feb—1 Mar 1945
- Manila Bay-Bicol Operations: Mariveles-Corregidor 14-28 Feb 1945; El Fraile (Fort Drum), Manila Bay 13 Apr 1945; Carabao Island, Manila 16 Apr 1945
- Borneo: Tarakan Island Operation 27 Apr—5 May 1945
- Okinawa Gunto Operation: 5th and 3rd Fleet Raids in support of Okinawa Gunto Operation 28 May—5 Jun 1945
- Third Fleet Operations against Japan: 10 Jul—15 Aug 1945

Other:
- ♦ Navy Occupation Service Medal (Asia) 2-3 Sep 1945
- ♦ Philippine Republic Presidential Unit Citation Badge: 18-29 Oct 1944; 7-8 Dec 1944; 12-18 Dec 1944; 4-18 Jan 1945; 14 Feb—1 Mar 1945; 12 Apr 1945; 16 Apr 1945

ADMIRAL WILLIAM F. HALSEY SPEAKS

In his Foreword of *Action Tonight* by James D. Horan, Fleet Admiral William F. "Bull" Halsey had this to say about the USS *O'Bannon*:

> The history of the Pacific war can never be written about without telling the story of the U.S.S. *O'Bannon*.
>
> Time after time the *O'Bannon* and her gallant little sisters were called upon to turn back the enemy. They never disappointed me.
> ...
> No odds were ever too great for them to face. They fought battleships and heavy cruisers; escorted vitally needed supply ships for marines on Guadalcanal; bombarded Japanese positions; aided in dangerous rescue operations; and derailed the Tokio Express so often that the Japanese admirals ran out of excuses.
>
> No medals, however high, can reward the gallant men of the tin-can fleet for their brave deeds.[3]

---

[3] Horan, James D. *Action Tonight*, New York, G. P. Putnam's Sons, 1945

Walter Allen Lee
Boot Camp, Norfolk, VA, 1939

CHAPTER 2

HAWAIIAN ISLANDS

By now, I had been in the Navy four years, and I had served on several ships. This account begins with my transfer to the destroyer USS *O'Bannon*.

§§§

3 February 1944
Pearl Harbor, The Hawaiian Islands

We arrived in the Navy Yard, and I was transferred to COMDESPAC FLEET. I stayed in the receiving station area one day and was transferred to the USS *O'Bannon*, DD450, a ship with a superior war record. I was told it sank nine ships and had ten Jap planes to its credit. (Of course, this may be a great exaggeration.) I came aboard expecting a snappy ship, but the communication system was a mess. We have a First Class Radioman who is excellent, but he does not know Navy. Maybe I can help.

8 February 1944
Pearl Harbor

I find myself on another training cruise. After all the dealings that this ship has had with the Japs, it is still doing training exercises. We go out to sea every day, but we do get to come into port in the evening and secure the Fox skeds with movies on the foc's'cle. We do get to read and write letters.

10 February 1944
Pearl Harbor

Well, I suppose this is "it." We received word today that we are to join a task force for a little action. Action will test my strength and character, etc. Or, in other words, a test to see if I have the guts. I may be going to my death, but there won't be much lost. After looking over my diary, I see myself as a pretty small-minded, conceited individual, with no thought of anyone but myself. Hopefully, that is in the past.

There is so much I want to do and so much that I want say, but I just don't know how. If Jesus tarries, these words in my diary will provide my future encounters with the Japs. Everybody is raving about the Japs, but I question if all those who write know very much about them, except that their performance in the past proves them to be crafty and sneaky as hell—or, is that propaganda?

As I look over my past, which is filled with a lot of rotten experiences, which I called fun, I haven't found what I am looking for—that is, contentment and happiness. Who doesn't? I do want to get married to someone I really love without being cynical about her. I want children of my own. I do have faith in prayer. Why shouldn't I pray? Maybe I will pray more often in the very near future. What I want is in God's hands whether my life will end in this war. I have led a wasteful, but full life. If it is God's will that I die, I pray that I will go to Heaven, but how can I, unless I have faith in Him, and take my troubles to Him? I must quit and write the necessary letters..

11 Feb, 1944
En route to the Marshall Islands

One thing good about this ship is that we are told where we are going, and the Captain lets us in on confidential war news with his speeches on the speaker system. We are escorting a unit of four transports to the Marshall Islands. This "tin can" is the only escort ship. I have never known the Navy to put so much faith in one destroyer before. I suppose it is necessary since the rest of the Navy is fighting a war. I am kind of anxious to get into this scrap and get it over with, one way or the other. We have no choice but to be successful! It looks like my wishes will be granted "cause we sho is headed thataway." The latest dope is that we lost 300 men in the Marshall Islands, and the Japs lost 8,000 men, so far. Nice going, if it is true?

One of the Crew, USS *O'Bannon*, World War II

I have come to the conclusion that I am fighting this war more for myself than anyone else. I want to get it over with, and do my share to end it. It doesn't look like the folks who are safe in the homes in the States give a hoot about the military, according the news reports. My impression, at least.

We are on a smooth sea with a beautiful moon. Makes a guy wish for things.

CHAPTER 3

MARSHALL ISLANDS

18 Feb 1944
Majuro Bay, Marshall Islands

We stayed at General Quarters (manned all battle stations) from 0100 'til daybreak, then pulled into port at 0800 this morning. This Bay is full of ships; three battleships, mostly supply ships and tankers. I slept most of the day, and don't think anything happened while I was asleep.

We just received a message to take 13 two-thousand bombs to Tarawa. We will leave soon, and I do hope we don't run into trouble with all that that aboard!

21 February 1944
Majuro Bay, Marshall Islands

Our visit here has been most pleasant. We have a swimming party every afternoon off the fantail. It is lot of fun, and we have movies on the fo'c'sle every night. This is the way to fight a war! There does not seem to be any opposition here. There are no Jap planes in the air, and our Navy can't find any Jap ships. The Battleships are constantly bombarding Wotje (Marshall Islands) and other Jap positions. The way they took this place is a joke: They bombarded this island atoll for days, and our planes dropped bombs on it. When they landed ashore, there were only three Japs on the whole atoll. There isn't much land, just a small strip of land surrounding the bay. It once, I was told, had been a volcano, and the surrounding land is all that is left. We have the harbor patrol tonight.

One of the Crew, USS O'Bannon, World War II

23 Feb 1944
Majuro Bay, Marshall Islands

Today was payday, and I have $200.00, but no place to spend it. We went swimming over the side today, and I needed the exercise. Bowman, the first class, has put me in charge of all communications and radio central. My training on the *Pokomoke* makes this job a simple one. I have all the Navy files in good shape. I am taking the algebra course, which is coming back to me. God only knows when I will use it. I am really beginning to like this ship. It isn't like the old Navy, but these guys are doing it pretty well their way.

26 February 1944
At sea

We are escorting the *Nassau Bay*, a ship converted into a Carrier, from Majuro on her way back to Pearl Harbor.

We left the *Nassau Bay* as it joined three other carriers and a group of destroyers, and we should be back in Majuro Bay tomorrow morning. I like our Communications officer, LT Thomas Timothy Murphy, and we have a fine group of officers on this ship.

29 Feb 1944
Majuro Bay, Marshall, Islands

We arrived to find to what looks like the whole U. S. Navy in the harbor: 12 battleships, 9 Aircraft Carriers, about 15 cruisers, and 20 or more destroyers. That is one big mess of ships to be seen all at once in one place. The *Lang*, DD399, my old ship, is also in the group of "Tin Cans." Scuttlebutt has it that we will make an assault on Truk (Caroline Islands)! I don't think it will be a landing, as this is one big Jap base. I want to get in on the action, and be some kind of hero. Just finished a letter from my mother telling me she is praying for me day after day, and she wrote that she knows I will be safe if the world is! The Japs cannot win this war! I feel ready for some stateside duty. I suppose I am suffering from the second stage of home sickness.

Marshall Islands

I am doing my best to square away this Radio Shack and the Radio gang to teach them the Navy way of operating efficiently as I was taught. So far, I do have their attention. I had to hit one of my men the other night, but he asked for it. After I flattened him, I have had the very best cooperation. If necessary, I will take the method further. Mr. Murphy has entrusted me with all the Confidential files. After four years in the Navy, I should be competent.

1 March 1944
Majuro Bay

We are in port and we are at peace, I don't feel in a good mood nor a bad one. I was thinking of post-war days, and who all will claim to have won this war. Win it, we will! All of our American citizens are not really involved in winning this war, in my estimation. What doesn't hurt them, doesn't bother them. The suffering of other people does not mean a thing. When they see our Army or Navy on parade, they cheer, and it is a pretty sight. They also cheer when they see Lana Turner or Clark Gable. The little stories told by individuals involved up to their necks in the war doesn't mean a thing! Maybe I am a bit cynical, but this is a crazy world, and maybe I am a little crazy also. However, I feel that people care less about a man who risks his life a few times, and sees others die— for what? Most people are not grateful. They want to live in peace, make money, and are interested only in their own future. So, who wants their gratitude anyway? I could go on and write about my own petty feelings, but I know that I am a small cog in a very big wheel, and you have to be a big cog to get the most oil. (I didn't realize that I had such morbid thoughts.)

5 March 1944
At sea

We are getting some lousy duty. We are now escorting an empty ammunition ship to join a convoy going back to the States or Pearl Harbor. We have escorted the *Nassau Bay*, a "Jeep" carrier from Majuro, to join another convoy on its way back to Pearl Harbor. At least the sea is smooth, nothing like the North Atlantic or the North Pacific off the Aleutian Islands. We read everything we can get our

One of the Crew, USS O'Bannon, World War II

hands on, even the radio equipment instruction manuals, and I have been reading the Bible, which my mother presented to me on my last leave over two years ago. What a hopeless sinner I am! Mail from home has been hard to come by, and the mail we send is censored. We cannot write where we are, etc. I wouldn't like anyone reading my letters home anyway.

(A word about the "Jeep" carrier. These small aircraft carriers were escort carriers. The press called them "baby flat tops." They ended up just being called "Jeeps." Many were built by the Kaiser-Frazer Corp and came to be known as "Kaiser's Coffins." They performed well, but their pilots had problems landing their planes on the small decks in rough weather. One instance that I remember was when we were in the China Sea. A few guys were passing a football on the deck. One guy went for a pass—and kept on going—into the drink! We picked him up, and he still had the football!!!

In 1940, the Willys-Overland Company began building an all-purpose or general-purpose vehicle for the Army. It is believed that the word "Jeep" developed from "general purpose", which, when slurred together, sounds a bit like Jeep.)

Still escorting the ammunition ship. We had a submarine contact today, which is nothing unusual. We gave up after searching for about an hour. I am really getting my sea duty. For once in my naval career, I am really bored. I have never been so far from civilization before, and one feels so lonesome.

6 March 1944
At sea

With this time on my hands, the books I read and the news I listen to, and the news we copy by Reuters News Agency, gives me some impressions about this war. It seems that the people in the U. S. are fighting the Japs only in their minds and what the Japs did to us at Pearl Harbor. It seems that we have some political rats in the U. S. causing labor strikes and general upheaval. It's hard for me to fathom. Why, for God's sake! However, I will continue to fight this war without passion or hate towards the enemy, and hope it will end soon. We will win it if our government doesn't collapse. Roosevelt must be reelected. He knows the score, politically and otherwise. Let him end what was started on his watch.

Gad Zooks! I can think of the dumbest things to babble about on paper. I will change the subject and write about this Radio Gang. I have never known a navy radio gang like it. They are a lot of kids, very un-navy, except Bill Bowman, First Class, and Bob Butler, Third Class. Bill Bowman, at about twenty-eight years old, was at one time a Banana Boat radio operator and HAM, then he became manager of one of Boston's leading hotels, the Statler. He knows radio and has a pleasant personality.

Robert Honaker, from a small town in Virginia, is just a kid and is ambitious, wants to be promoted. He did get awarded Second Class Radioman, but in my view, does not deserve it.

John Cutler is a big guy from Chicago. Hard to figure out, but has a keen sense of humor. Noses into other people's business, but I like him, and we get along.

Harold Miller, Third Class, with an excellent background. A former bank employee, teller, etc. Has a wife and cute baby. Here is one clean-living guy, which I hope the Navy doesn't spoil. We have had a brief run-in, but I like the guy.

Bob Butler, a witty guy from Oklahoma, is a former baker for Wonder Bread. He is an okay guy and good company. He is a good radioman and a member of my watch.

Harry Hiller, Third Class. Here is a guy with self-pityitus. He thinks he is doomed to die. I had to knock him on his fanny one night. Everyone in the gang said he was hard to get along with, but since my incident, we have had no trouble. He does his duty well as a member of my watch. He is always complaining about his ears or something else. I think he wants to be transferred to a hospital.

One of the Crew, USS O'Bannon, World War II

George Boyte isn't very well liked by his shipmates because he is an "ear banger," and our worst radioman. He does small favors for me, and I don't know why. He caters to the officers, and has done all right. He was promoted to Third Class before he was qualified, and still isn't, in my view. Boyte and Hiller hate each other, and that is the one reason why I had to slap Hiller down. We must get along.

Mr. Thomas Timothy Murphy, our Communications Officer, is an ex college professor of Economy and Banking, and has more than one degree. He is like one of the radio gang; he is with us all the time. He is twenty-five years old. He seems to be a timid type of guy. (There are other members of the radio gang, but my watch was over, and my future writings were about other subjects.)

13 March 1944
Majuro Bay, Marshall Islands

We sailed in and tied up alongside the destroyer tender *Prairie*. I saw her burn fiercely off Argentia, Newfoundland in September, 1942. Okay now though. We secured our communications, which we turned over to the *Prairie* radio gang. It gave us a brief rest.

We are now back at it. We left the side of the *Prairie* and are at anchor. Bob Butler and I have the duty, and the rest of the gang is at the movies. When I was describing the Radio gang, I left out Mr. Charles T. Boning, the Assistant Communications Officer. He is my instructor in algebra. A swell fellow.

17 March 1944
At sea

We left Majuro Bay on the 14th, heading for the South Pacific to join our Destroyer Division 21 for duty, which remains a question mark. We crossed the equator today and had the celebration and the usual "Shellback" celebrations and initiations. I crossed the equator a few years ago while aboard the *Lang*. So I was initiated then, in the barber's chair. Some of these guys' haircuts are a mess. I had the watch, so I missed some of it. Lucky Lad! There hasn't been much to happen in these last few days, and it is getting monotonous riding this little sun-cooked tin can. All we can do now is hope for something to wake us up, and I am sure we won't be surprised.

CHAPTER 4

SOLOMON ISLANDS

18 March 1944
Purvis Bay, Tulagi, Florida Island Group, Solomon Islands

Here we are where man's life was cheap. This bay has a nickname, "Iron Bottom Bay." Because so many ships were sunk here. It is beautiful country, but who likes beautiful country under these circumstances? We steamed right up the "Slot." It is a body of water about 16 to 20 miles apart from the Islands, right up to Guadalcanal, which is much larger than I thought. It is a solid mass of blue beauty with clouds hanging over the mountain peaks. All this killing has added up to the saying, "what fools these mortal be." A guy gets awfully lonesome out here, cut off from the rest of the civilized world, imprisoned on this little ship, with few comforts except for movies, and candy, when we can get it. We all want peace, and we don't like the idea that we must kill other men to obtain it. Some of us have found that there is no sport in doing that. I wonder sometimes if I am afraid to die? However, it is a question of kill or be killed! Somehow, I feel that God has a better place for me. One might envy me for seeing all of this world that I have seen in my travels, but little would they know why it was done and how I hate it. However, I am proud to be a part of being involved to bring peace to my country. I am also proud of this little ship and its record—but she certainly has an independent crew.

[The *O'Bannon* reported for duty with Rear Admiral W. L. Ainsworth's task force on 18 March 1944, Purvis Bay.]

19 March 1944
Purvis Bay

Wow! It sure is hot here. The surrounding mountains knock off the wind. I don't think the Captain will keep us here long .

Brief interruption here—I am on the mid-watch with a cup of coffee to keep me awake. Got a bit of sound advice from Ensign Haynes, the son of a judge in Tennessee. One that I won't forget: "There is good in the worst of us, there is bad in the best of us, so who are we to judge the rest of us?"

That is something that applies to my everyday life here on this ship, as we are so closely associated.

27 March 1944
Purvis Bay

Still here, but I think we are going out to sea for a training session tomorrow. Everything has been going along smoothly these past few days with no friction. I hope it stays that way.

28 March 1944
At sea, Solomon Islands area

We steamed up the scenic "slot" from Purvis Bay with our entire task force 38, which includes our Destroyer Division 21 and three cruisers, *St Louis*, *Honolulu*, and *Birmingham*. The destroyers as I can name them are: *O'Bannon*, *Nicholas*, *Hopewell*, *Taylor*, and *Fletcher*. That is all that I can name. The *Hopewell* and *Taylor* have excellent battle records.

We held antiaircraft firing, and the *O'Bannon* was the only ship to shoot down the sleeve. Damn good shooting! LT(j.g.) Huck and his fire-control crew do well. I am proud of this little ship, even though I did not participate in its previous battle experiences.

28 March 1944
Purvis Bay

Here we are back again. Will we ever get involved in this war? We tied up alongside the *LaValette*. It and the *Jenkins* are also members of Division 21, which I didn't mention as taking part in the practice. The *O'Bannon* crew is different from those on other ships; we don't paint Jap flags on the stacks, and the other ships do.

One of the Crew, USS O'Bannon, World War II

The *LaVallette* has 10 Jap flags on one of her stacks for Jap planes they have bagged. Our guys treat the LaValette crew with scorn because of this, but it is only skin deep.

29 March 1944
Purvis Bay, Tulagi

We came into port and tied up alongside the *LaValette*, another destroyer in our Division. The *Radford* and *Jenkins* are two other ships that I did not mention in naming Task Force 38. We secured the watches on a four-hour basis, as we split them with the *LaVallette*. The *O'Bannon* crew will not agree to paint Jap flags on the smoke stacks to show her victories over the Japs as other ships do.

[Editor's note: Is it possible that the Japanese spared this ship, or chose other targets because the *O'Bannon* did NOT have the "kills" painted on their smokestacks?]

5 April 1944

Received news today that the *O'Bannon* has been awarded the Presidential Unit Citation, and that its Captain, Donald MacDonald, is the most-decorated man in the Navy. (We later learned that his award for this was being made an Admiral and appointed as the Commanding Officer of the USS *Williamsburg*, the President's yacht. I met the Admiral at the Myrtle Beach, South Carolina reunion in 1987, and played in the same golf foursome with him and LT Swartz. I have forgotten the name of the other player in the foursome. I did my share of "ear banging" when I came up with a fifth of vodka from the trunk of my car—the Admiral likes screw drivers.)

We are shoving off tomorrow for a destination unknown, but as a radioman, we learn the "scoop" early on. We are going to Milne Bay, New Guinea. They say it is the hottest place on earth.

CHAPTER 5

NEW GUINEA

6 April 1944
At sea, en route to Milne Bay, New Guinea

We are off to where we will perhaps be involved in fighting this war. Maybe we can relieve the boredom and see some action. I forgot to mention that when at Guadalcanal, Mr. Murphy, Bill Bowman, and I went ashore to pick up a very-high-frequency radio set. We were there for the day with hardly any food to eat. I saw a few Marines lying around in the dirt. They were a dull-looking group, staring off into space. I think they had had it pretty tough. There were trucks, airplanes, boats, and Jeeps—all running. Now I know where all the nation's gasoline is. On the way ashore, there was a black native riding in the boat with us. He looked like a guy in one of those African Safari movies. He did not have a bone in his nose, though.

9 April 1944
At sea

We left Milne Bay this AM, and are on a scenic trip close to land at 25 knots, on our way to Buna, New Guinea. Buna is an advanced base, and we will have three days' practice operations with the Army. We aren't supposed to meet up with the enemy, but it is possible.

10 April 1944
At sea, off New Guinea

We are cruising with a lot of LSTs full of "Aussies" and American troops, practicing invasion tactics—all practice. Mr. Murphy tells us that we will be doing the real thing shortly. The place we are to bombard is Wewak, Papua New Guinea, and we are also to land troops there. It's to be one of the biggest landings launched in the

Pacific. This is our chance to see a little action. We have seen some beautiful scenery in this part of the world—surrounding blue mountains with clouds surrounding the tops, and the evenings with a gorgeous moon. I am sick and tired of beautiful scenery. Let's get on with the war!

16 April 1944
Sudet, New Guinea

I have heard several "sea stories" told by those who were in the Guadalcanal operation. This one was told to me by Bill Bowman:

It has to do with a "soft-hearted" Squadron Skipper by the name of Captain Ryan aboard the *Nicholas*. The Japs were trying to reinforce their troops on Guadalcanal by transporting troops from other islands using landing craft called "barges." DESRON 8 surprised them. There were no Jap ships to support the barges. Ryan ordered that the depth charges be fired from the "Y" and "J" launchers (for depth charges) that landed in the middle of the boats and killed Japs wholesale. Also, the 40mm guns to kill Japs. The barges would sink. If there were any surviving Japs swimming, he ordered depth charges to be set at shallow depths and dropped from the fantail to kill more Japs. In one instance, there were five Japs in a life raft. They were ordered to come aboard and surrender. They refused—so Capt Ryan backed the ship down and killed them with the ship's screws (propellers). Quite a guy!

18 April 1944
At sea

What a surprise! Since we have been over here in this part of the world, we have not encountered any Jap aircraft, except a "Betty" (Jap reconnaissance plane) seaward, quite a distance away. We have seen a few of our own aircraft. The Japs are keeping tabs on us.

Well, this looks like "IT"! We are on our way to perform in an invasion. Finally, we are going to war. We are in a small group of LSTs and Marine transports. Scuttlebutt has it that the invasion will be at Wewak. We will know shortly. The Captain ("Snuffy Smith") came on the PA system and said that we can be proud of a bronze star on our service ribbon after this operation. He went on to say that this operation will be a major blow to the enemy as its supply lines will be out of commission. He said the *O'Bannon* will have a ringside seat as we will be only 2,000 yards from the beach during the whole show. However, we will be in a very dangerous position.

20 April 1944
At sea

Here we are cruising along at about 10 knots, and we have joined a force of eight "Jeep" aircraft carriers, a few cruisers, some subchasers, a number of destroyers, and lots of landing craft. My General Quarters station was changed from the Emergency Radio Shack to Secondary Controls on the afterdeck. So, I will have a box seat for the whole show.

22 April, 1944
At sea, off the coast of Aitape Area and Hollandia, New Guinea

I feel much better now, although I missed two meals during today's action. I will provide a blow-by-blow description of the whole thing as I saw and heard it. Here it is:

It was almost 0400 when we went to General Quarters. We went to GQ early because our radar man thought he saw a submarine on his scope, which turned out to be a small island. I got off watch at midnight and attempted to sleep topside, but a rain squall drove me below-deck. Bob Butler and I "shot the breeze" for awhile, and we decided to take a shower. There is a slight tension among the crew, and several of them were joking about it. I am sitting here groggily tuned in on 3000 KC, the scene-of-the-action frequency, straining to know what is happening.

0415: Robert Honaker and Harry Hiller are discussing how the Japs can possibly defend themselves from such overwhelming odds that we have. We have about two hours before the big show will go on the road. I am afraid I won't get to see much because I am sitting here with head phones on my bean. (Apparently my General Quarters station was changed as I won't have the "Box Seat" which I had hoped for.) Maybe I can pick up some "hot dope" here on this action circuit. I don't think we will be entirely ignorant of what is about to occur. There are five of us on duty here in the Radio Shack. Robert Honaker, Jack Miller. John Cutler, Harry Hiller and myself. John Cutler suggested that we type *The Lord's Prayer* for practice. I told him to type it, make carbon copies and distribute them. Each of us should *say* the prayer!

0450: I will try reading something. This waiting is a pain in the neck.

0458: We turned on the Fathometer, which means we are nearing the beach. Bill Bowman just came in and advised that one of the minesweepers almost took a fish (torpedo). Evidently the Japs won't be idle. Bill said he had been watching the radar screen and expected to see a minesweeper missing (gone) every time he took a reading.

0536: Zero hour is drawing near. I feel like I used to when I boxed in high school—on pins and needles; that nervous, empty-stomach feeling.

0600: Here we go! Fired the first salvo of the 5-inch guns. This ship is doing a snake dance. Our guns were the first to fire. I looked at Harry Hiller, and his face was as white as a sheet. Maybe mine was too.

John Cutler is on the "skeds" (continuous flow of messages in Morse code). Miller went back to the Emergency Radio Shack to tune in on the task force frequency. Every radio frequency was manned. I haven't heard anything yet. It is hell to be here and not know what is going on. All of us are most serious and tense.

There go the 40mm guns! The acrid powder fumes are coming through the air vents. There go the foc's'le turrets (5-inch guns).

New Guinea

This bulkhead is fairly leaping back at me. After the bombarding, the planes will go in and strafe. Nothing to report on the circuit.

0611: There is a lull in the firing. We are probably circling for another run. Miller is nervously clipping his finger nails, and Hiller is efficiently smoking a cigarette. Cutler is calmly copying the skeds.

More firing! The more firing we do, the calmer I become. Miller commented that he would like to see the planes do their thing. The ship shakes from bow to stern while firing all its guns.

0635: There is another lull in the firing, and we are joking now. All seem more relaxed.

0642: The 40mm guns are going to town! Bob Butler came in and said the Japs are firing back. We must be close to the beach as the 20mm guns are also firing. There go the "cease firing" horns.

Firing again! Everything we have. Butler relieved me so I could take a peek outside. There was an awful lot of smoke. Our planes were dive bombing and strafing all installations, and doing it in pairs. The first wave of landing craft is on its way ashore, and the planes are really giving them hell.

We are close to the beach now, and it is obvious that the Japs have no big guns to fire at us. LT Thomas Timothy Murphy came in to tell us that all was going well, without a hitch. I went outside again and saw that they got one of our planes. He pulled out and glided down to a landing. It made the other pilots plenty sore. About eight planes went down firing. Evidently the Japs have MM guns and machine guns in one spot. I could see the tracers from the Japs guns firing.

Our LSTs are on their way in now, loaded to the gunwales. Quite a sight to see. I would hate to be a Jap. They are really catching hell. Our crew is all over the topside taking in the show. Everybody is calm now, no tension. It is now up to the troops to do the mopping up job. We will be around here for about four more days.

On our deck are shell cases all over. Bombarding is still going on farther down. The last wave of landing craft is on its way. The Japs tried to use machine guns and rifle fire to no avail.

Just helped Bill Bowman eat a wiener sandwich—-a helluva thing for breakfast. Mr. Murphy came and gave us each an apple. If our future battles go as well as this one, I won't mind a bit.

The battle isn't quite over. I watched the planes bomb the two small islands just off the beach.

2215: All is not over yet, They are still bombarding down the beach from us, and the planes are bombing the islands. A TBF, a torpedo bomber, made a beautiful attack on an ammunition dump on the closest island. An awful sight.

After a shower and excellent chow, I had no trouble sleeping. This is our first phase of the war, and the second for the crew who were aboard in the Solomon Islands operation.

23 April 1944
Aitape, New Guinea area

This morning at daybreak our destroyers were bombarding at all points. We could have been excellent spotters for one destroyer. We could watch his tracer fire. We are patrolling up and down the coast looking for evacuating Japs. The *Jenkins*, one in our squadron, sank a Jap barge last night. The Japs are trapped. If he takes to the sea, our destroyers are there to pick him off. If he stays on land, the odds are against him, because the Army is all over and moving in. The latest report is that 69 Americans lost their lives, and there were some wounded. Eleven hundred Japs were killed, and only three prisoners were taken. The planes bombed and strafed objectives well within our view. They made direct hits too. A fuel dump went up in a cloud of smoke.

New Guinea

We received word at 2200 hours that the Japs had made a bombing run on Red Beach, about 150 miles from here. So, we may well expect an attack tonight or early in the AM. There were three invasions designated as follows: Blue Beach, White Beach, and Red Beach. The places in order are Tanah, Merah, and Humboldt, which is our beach. We have a couple more days here. We are acting as fighter director for the planes. No Marines were in this show. Only the Army and the Navy.

We could see the airstrip at Aitape, and there were an awful lot of wrecked Jap planes. I thought the planes did one helluva job, but could hardly believe they destroyed that many planes. [I saw on the History Channel that B-24s, escorted by P-38 fighters, had bombed the hell out of that airstrip and destroyed "piles" of Jap aircraft, which explains why we had no air contacts or problems with them while in the New Guinea area.]

24 April 1944
Aitape, New Guinea Area

We are still patrolling. A lot of people were gathered around a former Mission and Hospital. We thought they were Japs, and we started to open fire, but it turned out that they were our own soldiers.

We passed one of those islands that was bombarded, and the planes bombed and strafed. There was a terrible sickening smell. The wind was in our direction, and we had to turn off the ventilators. Ripe, rotting human flesh doesn't agree with me. I think we have one more day of patrolling.

28 April 1944
At sea

Well, it finally happened. A group of Jap bombers flew right across our bow and bombed the beach, destroying a lot of supplies and nearly sank the *Etamin*, a Liberty ship. It was full of supplies and manned by Coast Guard sailors. Another Liberty Ship is towing the *Etamin,* and we are escorting them at five knots. If a Jap sub doesn't pick us up, it will be a miracle.

Sudet, New Guinea

Last night, the other patrolling destroyer was fired at by two Jap torpedo planes. Both "fish" missed. We just arrived in port tonight at Sudet, New Guinea. The Jap bombers returned to Aitape and did quite a bit of damage at Aitape according to reports.

7 May 1944
En route to Milne Bay, New Guinea

We had been lying in port for the past couple of days. Swimming in the afternoon and movies in the evening. We are on our way to pick up the mail for our squadron. I still haven't received my Christmas packages.

To change the subject. When a fellow reads about these invasions, which means that men die, and to see the pictures, he knows that war is a terrible thing. The newspapers make things look pretty good, but a map of the Pacific shows that we have advanced very little. Man, this war will be the end—who knows—besides God!

8 May 1944
Milne Bay, New Guinea

We arrived here this morning and picked up the mail, but not one single letter for the *O'Bannon.*

11 May 1944
At sea

We left Milne Bay with the rest of our squadron and ten LSTs.

12 May 1944

We pulled into this beautiful little harbor this morning. It is a copra plantation—or was one. It still looks like it is in pretty good shape. P-39 and P-38 planes have been swooping around us, showing off! We learned that we will be shoving off for Noumea, New Caledonia, to officially receive the Presidential Unit Citation, presented by Admiral Halsey[4]. That isn't far from Australia—maybe we will go there for some R&R??? All of our destroyer division is with us except the *Jenkins* and the *Taylor*. There is the *Nicholas,* that has our Division Commander aboard, the *Hopewell, Radford, Fletcher* and the *LaValette.* No one knows why all of us are traveling together. Maybe duty in the Indian Ocean?

---

[4] Admiral William Frederick "Bull" Halsey, five-star admiral of the U. S. Navy (Fleet Admiral)

CHAPTER 6

NEW CALEDONIA—AND BACK TO THE SOLOMON ISLANDS

14 May 1944
Noumea, New Caledonia
Oceania, islands in the South Pacific Ocean, east of Australia (between Australia and Fiji)

Here we are in a beautiful harbor with some beautiful weather. It's warm in the daytime and cool enough for a blanket at night. I haven't been ashore yet, but those who did go came back to the ship stewed to the gills. None for me, thanks.

We all are trying to figure out why we have the whole destroyer division down here? Maybe we will be transferred to another war area? We did receive mail. It has been a while. The scuttlebutt is that we may transferred to the East Coast to try our hand in that war with Hitler.

Butler, Miller, and I went ashore and attended a church. The church was small. The pastor was an Army Chaplain. The congregation was full of servicemen. The sermon was entitled, "The Lord's Prayer." It was a good sermon, and we felt good by attending.

23 May 1944
At sea

We departed Noumea at about noon today, and we are headed for Treasury Island (Solomon Islands), or Bougainville (Papua New Guinea). This little ship is really getting around. By the way, Halsey didn't show up for the presentation. I am sure he was too busy for that! When we were told about liberty in Noumea, we were warned not to drink any of the Brandy, because it was made from aviation gasoline. (Censored) came back too drunk to walk. Today, he said he would like to go back and fuel up!

25 May 1944
At sea

Still en route to Treasury Island off the coast of Bougainville. We are off to our next operation to silence some shore batteries and Jap installations. "TT", Thomas Timothy Murphy, our communications officer, says it will be dangerous. One never knows. While out here, I want to do all I personally can to end this war, because once I leave, I will never come back. My morale has taken a licking.

26 May 1944
At sea

We made the scenic journey up "the slot" into Tulagi to pick up mail and freight for our squadron, while the *Nicholas* picked up mail in Purvis Bay (Solomon Islands). We picked up only one letter for me, and the *"Nick"* picked up 36 bags of mail for the *O'Bannon* alone! Oh, Boy!

We left Tulagi on a sea of glass. I wish I could describe one of these sunsets. They are really beautiful. Every day I tell myself that I am sick of all this scenery, but my eyes are wide with awe when I see it.

We are on our way to Treasury and should arrive there at 0700. From there, I have no idea where we will go to knock out the shore batteries and Jap installations.

27 May 1944
At sea

Before departing Treasury Island, which is a very beautiful harbor, we were greeted by birds that came out to welcome us. We had a swimming party with the tropical fish off the fantail in that beautiful purple water in appearance, but clear.

We fueled up and are on our way to New Ireland (Papua New Guinea) to do our bombarding. I am not quite as excited and

One of the Crew, USS O'Bannon, World War II

enthused as I was at Aitape. Aitape was such a picnic. There were 3,000 Japs at Aitape. They knew we were coming, and the main force retreated to the mountains. After the landing, they attacked. It was do or die, and they must have died, because I am not aware of any major losses (on our side), according to Reuters.

29 May 1944
Treasury Island

We have just returned from bombarding Jap positions on New Ireland Island. The following is my observations while doing our duty:

Midnight: Time for General Quarters is drawing near. Since I couldn't sleep, I went up on the bridge and joined Flood and Murray. Flood is a signalman and was on duty. One witty guy. We shot the breeze for awhile. Enough—let's get on with the show.

The *Nicholas* and *Hopewell* are going in first to try and draw enemy fire. We are not scheduled to go in until 0600, but we will if the *Nick* and *Hopewell* run into any trouble. We radiomen are manning quite a few circuits. Too many in my view. We have A. D. Chandler, the Squadron Commander, to thank for that. I am in the Emergency Radio Shack, my GQ station, and it is like a furnace in here. Before coming back, Miller wished me luck and said to give him a ring if I got scared. He was a little pale. I am not afraid; I trust the Lord and my mother's prayers will protect me. My job is to load the antenna on the TAJ (I have forgotten what those letters mean, but it is a radio transmitter to keep the receivers tuned in to it.) Gad! Is it hot! Butler called, and I told him I would give him a growl when the TAJ is hooked up.

They say the operation is exceedingly dangerous, and we will get shot at—maybe hit! The *Nick* is having trouble contacting one of the planes. I am listening to the radio, and the *Nick* is still calling the plane.

Miller relieved me, and I am now in Radio Central. The *Nick* is still calling the plane, which seems to be delaying the operation.

They have an auxiliary plane now, and the messages are being passed to it. Butler and I went out on deck, and we could see the *Nicholas's* and *Hopewell*'s tracers giving them [Japs] hell at close range. The plane was dropping flares to give them a target. We are supposed to make our run at 0610. I am sleepy and tired and almost fell asleep out on deck—almost.

0510: All ships and planes have established contact now. One more hour and it will be our turn. I don't think the *Nicholas* and *Hopewell* drew any enemy fire last night. If so, we would have heard. Our radio contact with them is excellent. I am so hungry, I am nearly sick. Everyone in our group is very calm right now. We have about 40 minutes to go.

0555: ALL HANDS MAN YOUR BATTLE STATIONS!

It means "wake up", because all hands have been on their battles stations all night. We radiomen must stay awake while others can sleep.

Went back to the Emergency Radio Shack to set up the antenna on the TAJ. Bowman had found a water bottle in the antenna trunk, which grounded the thing. It is getting daylight now, and we are moving in on the beach.

We should be opening up our firing at any second! There go some 20 millimeter fire from one of the other ships. All is silent here in the Radio Shack. No one seems to want to talk. Cutler is reading a magazine, Hiller is on the skeds, Miller has his head down on the supervisor's desk (Miller carries a life jacket wherever he goes), Boyte is on the task force circuit with eyes staring, and Honaker is sitting in the doorway of the radio shack stroking his brow. I am writing this with my feet propped up on the Fathometer. We are testing with the spotting plane.

0635: Nothing cooking. Honaker went back to the emergency radio shack to try his luck with the TAJ. Miller is writing an anniversary letter to his wife. He has a two-year-old baby girl. He keeps pictures of the baby and his wife always close at hand. I went down to the Combat Information Center (CIC) to relieve Bowman, who is going back to try to make the TAJ work.

The *Hopewell* is firing at an enemy landing barge. "T.T.", Thomas Timothy Murphy, our Communications Officer, is as nervous as an old woman. The Japs are now firing back at us. Being inside, I cannot tell how close they are to hitting us. The Captain is raising hell with the Executive Officer here in Combat. He says that Combat is not firing at the enemy gun flashes. The Captain yelled down to cease firing and for Mr. Simmons to take over control.

I came up to the Radio Shack, and Miller is white as a sheet and shaking like a leaf, but he is joking about it. We reported that we are firing at the gun flashes. The forward batteries (5-inch guns) just opened up. Cutler jumped like he was shot. Exciting, but who likes this kind of excitement?

The plane is reporting all of our shots for us. We must be having good results as the plane hasn't instructed us to change targets—just told us to change three degrees! Just came back to the emergency radio shack to monitor the RAL in order to receive all transmissions on every circuit. I opened the outdoor hatch to note that we are very close to the shore. There is smoke and dust everywhere, and we are circling for another run. Here we go again! We are blasting away. I can't see them firing at us with the naked eye. We must be too far away. We are going back in for another run. Control suggested that we switch to rapid fire, as we are on target. The "Old Man" yells down the speaking tube that, "I don't want rapid fire; I want precision fire."

Just checked firing!

Here we go again on another run. I am in Radio Central now and heard the 40-millimeter guns fire. Don't know what the target is.

Miller, Honaker, and I are discussing the war. Just made another run. While the observation plane is correcting the fire, we receive all of the conversations.

The Japs missed the *Taylor* with four close ones. From my frequent visits to the superdeck, this time I feel that we are doing a terrible job. It looks like every five-inch salvo is going in the water. We are still using pin-point precision, or experimental fire, to obtain a target.

We are doing much better now—just silenced a Jap machine gun. A few of its bullets came close to the ship. It isn't very exciting now. Miller left for the outside. He said it might do him some good—if he doesn't faint before he gets there (joke). Miller came back in scared silly. He said our guns scare more than the Japs. He and Hiller act about the same. Butler is a little white around the gills, but remains calm. These boys have been through a lot on the previous operations in the Solomons, so even a mild operation like this one scares them.

Went outside again, and we are right up too close to the beach. We could easily be under rifle fire. A machine gun opened fire on a PBY (Patrol Bomber; Y-code for the manufacturer, Consolidated Aircraft Company) plane. Our guys are searching for a target. The 40mm guns just fired.

This coconut plantation (Medina Plantation) was at one time a large disembarking headquarters—there go the 20mm. As I was saying, our PT boats were operating in this area and were fired upon by the Japs repeatedly. So, the brass decided to send us down to investigate and engage, along with the *Nicholas*, *Taylor*, and *Hopewell*. The commander is A. D. Chandler.

1 June 1944
Departing Treasury Island

Oh, Oh! This definitely "it"! The Japs have come out of hiding. A large force was sighted with no less than nine battleships. We got an urgent dispatch addressed to COMDESDIV 21 (us). The force was sighted by one of our submarines. It is possible that we can catch them with their pants down! We are proceeding at 30 knots. There were three Jap destroyers sighted about three degrees north of the equator, near the Celebes (Sulawesi, Indonesia). The Captain gave us this information over the PA system. He said there was an enemy force headed toward Wewak (Papua New Guinea), near Green Island. Now is the time for us to say our prayers; we are going after the three destroyers...

2 June 1944
Sub Hunt At Sea

Our destroyer hunt has obviously turned out to be a wild-goose chase. We had a talk from the Captain again, who told us he believed the destroyers went to Truk Island, a Jap stronghold, and they can expect heavy bombing by our planes. The Captain went on to say that we have been ordered to join an escort carrier division at dawn to hunt for submarines in an area of 180 miles north and south and 200 miles east and west. It is believed that the Japs have a line of submarines of not less than seven subs—maybe no more than three now, thanks to a DE division, particularly the DE *England*. She may have knocked out the four subs.

Admiral Halsey congratulated the *England* crew with these words, "May there always be an *England!*" He said we have taken a tremendous toll of Jap subs in the past two months. He went on to say that our supply lines are so long now that we don't have escorts for the convoys all over the world; therefore, the most successful method is to concentrate on sinking the subs at their source. I do hope we get some excitement. I hate submarine patrols; I did those on previous ships in the North Atlantic.

The American submarine sailors are doing one helluva job! We have one that remains submerged in Manila Bay in the Philippines—of course without the Japs being aware— and it notes the Jap ship activity, then goes outside the harbor to report by radio.

HOLD EVERYTHING !!!!

I was on the skeds and received a message to the 272 group—that's us! Got the dope! It gave us details on how to operate. We are not to use the transmitters under ANY circumstances. Make a wide scouting search, and if we find a Jap sub on the surface, fire three torpedoes set at six feet. If we have any sub contact, to report, Flash it (signal light) to one of the planes in the area.

Just learned that the *England* sank four Jap subs. I hope we can top that record. Back to our heroic subs—there is another one of our subs keeping an eye on Jap ship movements—and not attacking—in the daytime. Those boys down below deserve a lot of credit.

3 June 1944
On sub hunt

Just relieved a DE division. Hope we get a sub.

3 June 1944 (later)
Sub hunt

We are still on a sub hunt, creeping along in a scouting line of four destroyers: *Nicholas*, *O'Bannon*, *Hopewell*, and *Taylor*. We have had several underwater contacts, but they were probably fish. We did not drop any depth charges.

The Jap fleet is on the move now. We are getting Urgent messages on the skeds—to All Ships Interested in Current Operations. Aren't we all? This includes aircraft operations. More later.

4 June 1944
Sub hunt at Sea

We had a little scare. A Jap "Betty" TBMB plane came within three and a half miles of us, and the *Taylor* opened fire at it. We secured GQ early. It was evidently just snooping. Ha! We were secured for GQ, but we were called back. We opened fire on the Jap plane. It dropped bombs intended for the *Taylor*, but they missed, Thank God! Our Captain got back on the "horn" to tell us that we would be called back to GQ later in the day and tonight as we can expect an air attack at any time.

1800: It looks like the Japs are after us since we spotted that Jap "Betty" today. We are at GQ now and expecting an air attack from some Jap "Bogies" (code name for enemy aircraft). They seem to be keeping a close check on us without attacking. We are headed for a rain squall to avoid a bombing attack. This GQ caught me just as I was about to take a shower.

Last night, our planes sank two Jap destroyers and left one dead in the water. That was a report from Mr. Murphy after decoding a message. This sub hunt seems foolish to me. We are just looking for trouble. The Japs know our every move, and surely they will not put any subs in our path.

I went out on deck and watched the Jap observation plane circle us about twelve miles away. He made a complete circle of our ships as we waited for him to attack. He left, but I feel that it won't be for long. I think they will be back in force for a torpedo plane attack later on tonight. We are only about 400 miles from Truk, the Jap stronghold, and we believe the plane came from there. We should head for port, as we are wide open for an attack. We are still at GQ, and I hope we will secure soon, as I would like to finish my shower.

We just picked up another "bogey" on the radar. We gave its position to the other ships. It is now 1920 hours.

CHAPTER 7

ADMIRALTY ISLANDS, OR MANUS, PAPUA NEW GUINEA

6 June 1944 (D-Day in Europe)
Departing Manus Island (Admiralty Islands)

We went in for fuel and food supplies. We are headed back for the sub-hunting area.

The Captain announced tonight that our troops had invaded the northern part of France. May God make them victorious! Hiller was transferred today—back to the States for new construction (qualified radiomen are always in demand). I was sorry to lose him because it leaves us shorthanded. One fellow who left the ship to attend radio school in San Diego is returning. Zarnecki is his name.

7 June 1944
At sea, sub hunt

As yet, we have not found a sub, and I don't think we will. That "Betty" Jap plane spoiled our chances. The Japs aren't stupid and won't put any subs in our paths. Now that the allies have captured Rome and invaded France, and we have pushed the Japs back on this side, things look fairly good.

Just noticed in my past few days writings that I neglected mentioning that we have the "Jeep" or baby carrier, *Hogalt Bay*, with us. It carries mostly TBF Avenger aircraft. They are torpedo bombers. In addition, it has a few "Wildcat" fighter planes. They shot down a Jap Betty and sank a sub in the last few days.

We are in some lousy weather, rough with a heavy fog clinging over the water. I really feel sorry for the pilots that have to fly in it constantly. These guys are really being put through the mill. Two destroyer-escort destroyers joined us this morning.

One of the Crew, USS O'Bannon, World War II

10 June 1944
At sea, sub hunt

Every day is getting more monotonous for me. We are in a choppy sea, which gives us a maddening roll. Trying!

The Navigator tells us that we have crossed the equator nine times. There is scuttlebutt that we are going to Sydney, Australia, at the end of this month. This comes from the Signalmen. I have heard a lot about this place—the girls pursue the dates with our sailors.

The *Taylor* sank a submarine yesterday. There was no doubt about it. She dropped a pattern of depth charges which brought the sub to the surface, then she opened fire with every gun she has on the starboard side. The sub went back under. The *Taylor* dropped more depth charges, and it came up again bottom-up! Well, our efforts are bearing fruit after all.

God! I despise this duty! It is my pet hate. Day after day of monotony, slow speed, searching constantly for something that can't be seen. Oh, well, it won't be like this in '48! [I don't know why I made this remark.]

11 June 1944
Sub hunt at sea

Still on this monotonous duty. Bob Butler picked up an "SOS" last night on one of our emergency circuits. We didn't think much about it since the Navy does not use "SOS" any more. We did report it to the Commodore on the *Nicholas*. He reported it to the carrier. It sent out search planes and spotted two men on a life raft. The *Hopewell* was dispatched to pick them up.

"TT" Murphy told us that we would be leaving at dawn for Treasury Island. We had chicken for chow at noon today.

We were called to GQ for 30 minutes. We thought we had a "bogey", but it was a PBY on patrol. This Captain calls GQ for any out-of-the-norm situation. Some call him GQ Smith, and

38

others call him "Smiley" Smith. Our signalman Flood calls him "Snuffy" Smith. He is called "Smiley" because he is always smiling at nothing humorous. All I can say for him is that he leaves the "Radio Gang" alone, and, in my view, he is conscientious in everything he does, whether the crew likes it or not. This bunch of "heroes" resent him for some reason. He is a fine skipper in my view. He realizes we are at war, and he knows his responsibilities!

13 June 1944
Sub hunt at sea

Had some tough luck today. One of the torpedo planes on the *Hogalt Bay* crashed on takeoff. The crew perished.

We were called to GQ again as our radar picked up "Bogies." They were Army planes returning from a bombing run. I am anxious to know if they got the Jap cruiser and two destroyers that were in Truk area last night. We were waiting until they got closer to us before attacking them.

We will be relieved tomorrow by DESDIV 47 (destroyer division), then we will depart for Treasury, which will end two weeks of this boring duty.

14 June 1944
At sea

We are due into Treasury Island tomorrow morning. We have some unnecessary GQs today—practice 5-inch gun firing.

CHAPTER 8

SOLOMON ISLANDS

15 June 1944
Entering Treasury Harbor

The Captain gave us some pretty good "dope." He said we should have firsthand information: "before our good fellows back home do." He implied that we had taken the Mariannas, and our future operations would be west of New Guinea. He didn't say it directly, but we in the radio gang know that it has already happened. Also, we know that our fleet was in waters that the enemy never thought we would ever be in. He said the Jap fleet is getting restless and was moving in huge force to the west of New Guinea area. He added that we must be ready for an engagement with the Jap fleet in the very near future. Oh, Me!

16 June 1944
Treasury Island

Good news! Tokyo was bombed by our B-24 bombers, the plane with the 141-foot wing span. I wonder how many planes they used and to what effect was the damage?

17 June 1944
At sea

The "Squad Dog" (Squadron Commander) must hate the *O'Bannon*. He dishes out the rotten duty every chance he gets, while the rest of the squadron lies in port at Treasury. We have been assigned to escort a seaplane tender, the *Wright*, to Seaddler Harbor in the Admiralty Islands.

This "old man" is driving us all nuts with his "General Quarters." He is still being called "GQ Smith" by the crew. He seems to be edgy and contrary too often and chews out the officers, then they

Solomon Islands

come down on the crew. Bowman has his GQ station on the bridge, and he catches hell along with the officers. Bowman is walking around like he has lost his best friend. The Captain threatened to put Ensign Haynes, who is from Nashville, in the Brig!! (There is more to this story which I will omit.)

22 June 1944
Treasury Island

Arrived yesterday. I managed to get a full night's sleep. Admiral Nimitz[5] notified us that the Fifth Fleet had engaged the Jap fleet—we have no results.

LT Thomas Timothy Murphy gave the radio gang a typewritten memo that he expected every member to perform their duties with absolute perfection. It is so unlike "TT". It is apparent that he was instructed to do this by the "Ol' Man." This Captain is a Naval Academy graduate and all of the officers are Navy Reserve, and he wants to whip them into line. He has let them know that he wants nothing short of perfection in their duties.

Had two lousy movies on the foc's'cle this evening. We also had a movie short advising the power of our Japanese enemies. We have a long, long way to go before they are defeated, but it is going to happen!

23 June 1944
Treasury Island

We remain in port today, and the "Old Man" started the day off with General Quarters. It was an Abandon Ship drill, which he did not announce over the speaker system. We in the radio shack didn't know what was going on. The "Old Man" came into the radio shack mad enough to pop. He gave Murphy hell. He said we should scout around and find out what's going on. How can we scout around with us at GQ?? He is nuts! Mr. Murphy said he may be broken to apprentice seaman for telling him off some of these

---

[5] Admiral Chester William Nimitz, five-star admiral (Fleet Admiral)

days, and I can't blame him! The Captain is mercilessly giving every officer on the ship hell for such trivial, juvenile things. Judging from the rotten duty that we have been getting, it is obvious that the Squad Dog has been sick of him for some time.

My brother Frank is an officer with NATS (Naval Air Transportation Service) and is stationed in Oakland, California. My brother Norman is in the Army as buck private, and he has two kids.

25 June 1944
Treasury Island

We went to sea today to correct any damage control problems. I earned a feather in my cap for correcting an antennae problem. You would not be interested in the details.
Today is the *O'Bannon*'s second birthday! It called for a celebration. No booze allowed on any U. S. Navy ship. We had roast turkey, mashed sweet potatoes, giblet gravy, and all the trimmings.

Butler and I went over to the beach and had a few beers, looked over the graveyard, and went swimming with the pretty, colored fish.

We had a "happy hour." I had the watch and couldn't go, but I am told, we have a couple of comedians on board, and our musicians, "The Joe Pot Jivers," put on a good show. I am sunburned and tired, and have the long watch from Chow time to Midnight. We are tied up alongside the *Molijack*, a PT tender, to repair our sound gear. Being alongside a tender usually gives us radiomen some relief, as the tenders take on the communications responsibility, but not this time. We are maintaining all the radio circuits around the clock.

We will be getting underway shortly, for another practice run most likely. Most of us want some action. All of the previous apprehensions about being in combat are gone!

30 June 1944
Treasury Island

For the past few days we have been going out to sea for antiaircraft firing, Good shooting too! Our Fire Control group are becoming experts.

A few of us appreciate this kind of boring duty, but some of us would prefer to be winning the war. We are on a training cruise, like being on a "shakedown cruise." Sherman said that "war is hell." (Union General William Tecumseh Sherman, U. S. Civil War.) He was wrong! *Training for war* is hell!

We have a 4th of July party to be held on the beach. Beer and Bar-B-Q will be plentiful. The other day, Butler and I were in swimming, and there was an earthquake. Butler said no more swimming for him.

5 July 1944
Treasury Island

The squadron 4th of July party went off on schedule. Butler and I went over and swizzled as much beer as we could hold. We came back to the ship for the afternoon watch and, boy, were we sleepy! There were several boxing matches, foot races, Bar-B-Q, and of course, beer. We had a good time, considering.

We are going back to sea this morning for more drills and training exercises. God! I hate this kind of life!

Here I am at 2200 hours on watch. We were at sea for torpedo runs today. These training exercises have been named "USO duty," but, to me, it seems so boring. I had rather be in a danger zone for a bit of excitement. This reminds me of the "shakedown cruises" on my previous duty at Guantanamo Bay and Trinidad. Murphy tells us that we will be in Sydney, Australia, in the middle of August. Great news! We need some female companionship.

One of the Crew, USS O'Bannon, World War II

7 July 1944
Treasury Island

Except for the beauty of this island and the pretty fish, I am not too happy with this place. None of us are. We stayed in port until about 1830, and went to sea to operate with the PT boats. We stayed out until about midnight and went to GQ. There is a lot of dissension here in the radio shack. Miller and Butler do not speak to each other unless it has to do with business. Without going into detail, I feel that we have been too closely associated for too long a time practicing how to go to war. (I have omitted the incidents that make this so obvious.)

I am continuing with my news sheet by copying the Reuters news casts which are in Morse code. Butler and Bowman help in this regard, along with Joe Sweda in the Yeoman's office with the stencils and Gestetner Mimeograph machine. We are keeping up with the war news this way. What I need is a rest. My spirit has taken a licking. I am irritable, and I find it hard to suppress it.

CHAPTER 9

ESPIRITU SANTO, VANUATU, AND GUADALCANAL

10 July 1944
En route to Espiritu Santo, Vanuatu, South Pacific (New Hebrides)

We left for a cooler climate and, maybe, some rest and recreation when we get there, but I doubt it.

Later: Sure enough, our orders were changed.

11 July 1944
Koli Point, Guadalcanal

We arrived here about noon. The skipper has some old buddies here that he wants to see. Besides that, we have to swap some ammunition, then we will be off to Espiritu Santo. I am issuing my press news like I did on the *"Willie Dee"*. [My former ship, *William. D. Porter*]

15 July 1944
Espiritu Santo

Here we sit in a portable dry dock. All hands went over the side, including me, for some really dirty work. It brought back some not-too-fond memories of when I was a deck hand. I took the watch with Honaker, and we won't have to go over the side today. We will remain on watch until 2200 tonight, which will be well worth it. I hate to scrape and paint. This is an excellent, beautiful harbor, but as I said before, beauty doesn't mean much to me, unless it is a beautiful woman.

I have a problem with this Captain. Nothing seem to go right with him.

Bowman is a good radioman and radio technician. He made the highest mark in the squadron. The Captain read the report and said that it was good, but that until 99.99% efficiency is attained, he still has some work to do.

16 July 1944
Espiritu Santo, New Hebrides

We are finally out of dry dock. I went over to the destroyer tender *Briareus* and stood an all-night watch, as the tender is handling the communications, but we share the radio personnel. It really made me tired. I turned in this morning and slept 'til 4 this afternoon, took a shower, ate chow, and went to a movie. Not a good show but had one of my favorite actresses in it—Evelyn Keyes. I also like Kathryn Grayson—I really like all the female actresses. I think I will write a letter home.

18 July
Espiritu Santo

We got a four-day extension to repair our #2 gun mount (5-inch). We are still alongside the *Briareus*. We are staying in touch with a circuit that lets us know what is going on up North. It isn't too tough, we are watching good movies, good chow, and we are getting plenty of rest—and, yes, we are getting some recreation. I intend to play a set or two of tennis tomorrow. I bought a new wrist watch today. It is a Helbros; shock proof, water proof, etc., for $ 65.00. That's a lot of cabbage, but it is a dandy watch..

22 July
At sea

We are in some heavy weather now and on our way back to Treasury. The USO duty is over with, with one thing in mind—we will get our MAIL!!!!

I do hope the old Squadron Commander has been relieved. He got his orders before we left. We will be senior ship. We can then copy Fox skeds to suit ourselves.

23 July
At sea

For the first time in my Navy career, I think I have the ship that suits my temperament. With all my ups and downs that I have had aboard, I haven't really been depressed as I was on the *William D. Porter*. I liked the *Beale*, but I had been living a fast life and found it hard to adjust to a destroyer. I was satisfied on the *Pocomoke*, but that was a lazy man's duty.

Maybe after I see a little action, I will be satisfied with some soft duty. But, first I want some action! I am thoroughly sick and tired of training, training—day after day. I don't want to be a hero; I just want to relieve this terrible monotony!

CHAPTER 10

SOLOMON ISLANDS, DUTCH EAST INDIES AND NEW GUINEA

25 July 1944
Treasury, Solomon Islands

Today is my 23rd birthday. We are back in our little, beautiful rendezvous. More drills?

27 July 1944
Same place

Received a letter from my brother Norman, who is in the Army. He is a leader of men, which is of no surprise.

I went to a religious movie tonight, "The Song of Bernadette." It was wonderful movie, but Catholic. It did contain some food for thought. Throughout the movie, the crew are devout sinners, judging by their conversations. Hardly a sound could be heard. It captured every man's undivided attention, including mine.

31 July 1944
Treasury Island

The Bureau of Navy Personnel came out with an ALNAV message clamping down on rates. It makes no difference to me. If I survive this war, I feel that there is limited opportunity in the Navy, and feel that I can do much better on the outside. The money is meaningless.

1 August 1944
Treasury Island

This new Squadron Commander is a man after my own heart. No training drills! The days are still dull. I had rather be in Saipan fighting the war. No mail lately, only a few "V" mail letters.

2 August 1944
Treasury Island

We are going to leave this area. We are to escort the merchant ship *Extavia* to Finschhafen, New Guinea. The *Taylor* is going also.

3 August 1944
At sea

I was wrong about our destination. Just shows how unpredictable our lives are. We escorted the merchant ship to the mouth of the harbor at Manus Island, and we are on our way back to Treasury. Butler and I are not on speaking terms with "T.T." Murphy. Butler knocked Miller down for some reason. The bad blood came to the boiling point between these two.

4 August 1944
Treasury Island

We arrived about 1800 and learned that Bob Hope and his show were over on the beach. We went over, and the show was great, although we had to stand up during the show. Bob Hope's jokes were funny. Jerry Calona, Frances Langford, Patricia Thomas, Barney Dean and some jerk named Tony Romano were performers. Frances Langford sang three romantic, sentimental songs, and Patricia Thomas danced. Boy, oh Boy! What a doll! Jerry Calona and Barney Dean told jokes that went over pretty good. The CBs furnished music by a black band which was very good.

6 August 1944
At sea

Our duty at Treasury Island is over. We are to report to another base. We don't know where yet. There is the invasion of the Philippines sometime in the near future, and I won't mind a bit.

One of the Crew, USS O'Bannon, World War II

8 August 1944
Seaddler Harbor, Manus Island

We arrived early this morning to relieve another destroyer squadron, of which my old ship the *Beale* is one of them, so that squadron can go to Australia. I will miss the trip.

Butler fouled up the detail the other day. He failed to copy an important message because he didn't feel like it. As supervisor of the watch, I was held responsible. Butler has been berserk these past few weeks. The dull routine is taking its toll. He knocked Miller on his can because he didn't like the way Miller told him to turn down the volume on one of the speakers for one of the circuits. Our watches are being changed. George Boyte is now on my watch instead of Butler.

9 August 1944
Manus Island

Yesterday we were given immunization shots, and the majority of the crew have sore arms. I had a boil on my arm, and the shot made it better. We have a Pharmacist's Mate by the name of Harper. He handled all the sick bay complaints. The doctor on board complained that he went to Santa Clara University to be a surgeon, and he thought he would practice his profession if he joined the Navy. Now, he says, "all I do is treat Fungus gardens," so he lets Harper take care of them. (I do hope Harper reached his goal to be a doctor and took advantage of the GI Bill for a college education as I did. He was a dedicated guy.)

11 August 1944
Manus Island

We have reported for duty in Task Force 74 under an Australian Commodore on the Aussie cruiser *Shropshire*. His name is Collins. He paid a visit to our Captain today. A pleasant-looking guy. Murphy said our next operation would be soon. All of us on board need a change. All of us are restless and dissatisfied. We are tired of the dull routine. Commander Bell wrote a book called

Solomon Islands, Dutch East Indies and New Guinea

"Condition Red" about the hardships in the destroyer Navy. He wrote of not having liberty for five months. Ha!

12 August 1944
Manus Island

I made up the Sunday News *Scuttlebutt* today, explaining our progress in this war, with maps.

14 August 1944
Entering port, Manus Island

We went to sea with the new task force. Our new Commodore was favorably impressed with our high score in gunnery practice. Gad Zooks! These guys have had enough practice! We are to operate with a submarine today and return to port this evening. More Practice! These nightly GQs are really getting to me—never enough sleep.

17 August 1944
Manus Island

We are going to sea again to operate with a submarine. We are taking along an Army brigadier general and 20 soldiers. These guys are going to sea for recreation! That's funny!

Mail is hard to come by.

19 August 1944
At sea

We were going with the submarine today and received a message to return to port immediately, which we did, and received the good news that we would be leaving for New Guinea—Aitape, to be exact. I thought we had won the war in New Guinea, but apparently there are some Japs left, with no way to leave.

One of the Crew, USS O'Bannon, World War II

20 August 1944
Aitape, New Guinea

We arrived at about noon today and will spend the next four days bombarding Jap "concentrations"— whatever that means!

We could see our planes dropping bombs and hear gunfire over on the beach. So we still have Japs in New Guinea.

21 August 1944
Aitape, New Guinea

We sailed up the northern coast and fired 100 rounds of five-inch ammunition. We shot up some huts, a native-built bridge, and some wrecked barges that littered the beach. Honestly, it wasn't worth the ammunition, and this will go on for three more days!!! A waste of time, money and effort.

Artisani spoke to one of the soldiers that we had aboard for a visit. He said we should visit the front lines where there are about 40,000 starving Japs who come down from the hills in groups of about 1500 looking for food. He said the infantry let them come down so far to cut off their ability to retreat, then the artillery opens up on them. He said the ridge is covered with Jap bodies.

22 August 1944
Aitape, New Guinea area

We took along a group of Australians on our bombarding mission today. We shot up some native huts and small boats along the beach today with no opposition. Stayed at GQ all day and had the mid-watch (Midnight to 4 AM) last night, and I am plenty tired. Press news looks good. Japan bombed, and advances made in France. We are about to enter port now. I think I will call it a day.

23 August 1944
Aitape, New Guinea

We did well today. We went close to where the Japs are trying to form a defense. We followed the planes in. They destroyed supplies, tanks, and gun emplacements. Fires were still burning when we arrived. As we shelled the beach, there was all kinds of equipment, 20 to 30 planes destroyed, trucks, landing craft, etc. We did not see any people, but there were villages with huts and signs of people having lived there—or maybe still living there. The Army has taken a very few prisoners.

Common sense would tell the Jap leaders to surrender. Their situation is hopeless. The Japs have set up a defense on three small islands offshore. The territory on the mainland closest to the islands is rugged hills. This is where the Japs managed to break through our lines. Now they are in worst shape than they were.

24 August 1944
Aitape, New Guinea

We completed our bombardment today with a shorter GQ. We finished about noon. It was a rotten day for firing weatherwise. Rain and fog limited good observation spots. We are waiting orders from CTF 74 for our next destination. We need fuel and ammunition. Some of our guys went over to the beach and saw where a war had been fought. All had arms just in case. My thoughts are about what I will do after the war. My future will not be in the Navy.

25 August 1944
Humboldt Bay, Hollandia, New Guinea

This is a huge bay, and has every kind of supply ship in it, along with the CTF 74 on the *Shropshire* cruiser. Our next operation is being planned aboard the *Blue Ridge* (a communication and flag ship). All commanding officers and communication officers are attending the meeting tomorrow morning.

We are supposed to leave with the *Nicholas*, *Taylor*, and *Shropshire* for Manus Island tomorrow evening or the day after. The brass do not want too many ships in this harbor as there may be an air attack.

The "Old Man" pulled another one of his disciplinary tricks during a GQ the other day. He was giving one of the officers, Mr. Freetage, hell over one of the phone circuits, and one of the guys on that circuit laughed and said, "Let's get on the ball up there." The Old Man heard him and wanted him put on report. No one tattled, so he restricted six officers for 30 days, and made them hold a phone talker drill for all hands that man a particular battle circuit, which is about a dozen men, during the movie each night.

The officers who were restricted were doing the unheard of thing by expressing their feelings to the enlisted men, like, "It's like having us write on a blackboard, 'I am a bad boy' in kindergarten." Which is true. But, when officers talk about the commanding officer distastefully to enlisted personnel, something bad will happen! We will see.

27 August 1944
At sea

The *Shropshire*, *Nichola*s and *Taylor* are with us, and we are to arrive at Manus Island this morning.

Orders are in for our next operation, and I will be in charge of the communications in the Radio Shack. Bowman will be on the bridge manning the TBS (Talk Between Ships).

I edited our Sunday News *Scuttlebutt* with war progress maps and a couple of cartoons. I think our next operation will be to invade the Halmahera Islands in the Molucco group, which is on the northern coast of New Guinea. Murphy said we will be in "serial convoys," whatever that means?

28 August 1944
Manus Island

I believe we will be operating with the third fleet; Halsey's old outfit. When we arrived here, the bay was full of tankers.

Murphy said our job was going to be easy as our principal job was to convoy, which I hate, but if it ends this war, I am willing to do anything! Our group will be the *Shropshire*, *Nashville*, *Hopewell* and *Taylor*. There are several "Jeep" carriers and other ships in the harbor—I don't know their names.

29 August 1944
Manus Island

Remained at anchor today. I sunbathed and slept. Took over the watch from chow to midnight. Received mail. Some guys got transferred today—none from the radio gang. We are preparing for the next operation, which, according to Murphy, will be easy for us, but who knows; war is unpredictable.

30 August 1944
Manus Island

The destroyer division went to sea today for tactical maneuvers (more practice) and returned to port for a bum movie. Rambo Murray and I chatted about our future when we get out of the Navy. Didn't solve anything.

31 August 1944
At sea

We are underway today for sham battle exercises with the "limey" cruiser *Shropshire* in charge. The opposition is the *Nashville* in charge of another group. We were to sail around, and the teams would locate each other and illuminate with star shells. Neither side won—it would take an actual gun battle to determine that.
After the exercises are completed, we are to proceed to Humboldt Bay, Hollandia, New Guinea, and hang around until we get the

Citation, then go on the Halmahera invasion. A big convoy of tankers came into port this morning, We had a rather late GQ tonight (2 hrs and 15 minutes of valuable sleeping time). One thing I will do when I get home is sleep!

3 September 1944
At sea

We, *O'Bannon* and *Taylor*, got called back into port today to convoy five LSTs. The *Nicholas* and *Hopewell* will escort six more tomorrow.

We have a new executive officer, Jack Wiss, from Chicago, and a Navy reservist. As editor and chief of the Sunday News *Scuttlebutt*, I put out a good one this week, thanks to Joe Sweda in the Yeoman's office who typed the stencil for the mimeograph machine.

4 September 1944
Humboldt Bay, Hollandia, New Guinea

Arrived this morning with our LSTs. There are several destroyers, two communication ships, tankers and supply ships, but no other war ships except the destroyers. I suppose we will be awarded the Presidential Unit Citation as Admiral Barbey is aboard one of the communication ships.

5 September 1944
Humboldt Bay, Hollandia

We are in preparation for the Unit Citation. Admiral Barbey will make the presentation. I am advised that there will be news reporters from *Time* and *Life* magazines, plus a newsreel photographer.

This old man is a pain. He put out an order tonight that he did not want any enlisted men sitting in front of him at the movies. Navy regulations say that movies are for the crew, and officers are invited as guests (so I am told).

Solomon Islands, Dutch East Indies and New Guinea

7 September 1944
Humboldt Bay, Hollandia, New Guinea

We stood in a blazing sun in our white uniforms today to be presented the Presidential Unit Citation earned in the Guadalcanal operation. Admiral Barbey made a complimentary speech, as did our Captain. The *Radford* and the *Nicholas* are tied up alongside. Their crews attended the ceremony. Both those ships had received their citations previously.

After the ceremony, I went over to the *Schroeder* to visit an old buddy of mine, Benny Benson. We served together aboard the *Pokomoke*, and we went on liberty together many times in Boston. He said he had been out in this part of the world 14 months with no liberty. We exchanged home addresses.

8 Sept 1944
At sea

I went over to the *Dobbin* and had a tooth pulled this afternoon, Didn't hurt, but my face is plenty sore. We had two movies on the foc's'le. I sat through one of them and then hit the sack. When I was awakened for the mid-watch, we were underway for Maffin Bay escorting a number of LSTs. I don't know how many.

10 Sept
Humboldt Bay, Hollandia

Returned from Maffin Bay last night before the movies. The trip was pleasant. I edited the press news with help from John Cutler, who helped with the typing, and George Boyte ran it off on the mimeograph machine. I have a "Snipe" drawing the cartoons. Reuters provides the news. I make the maps showing the Allied advances, then make a summary of the weekly news. I have a "home news" column and the "news today" to start the first page. Not bad, if I do say so myself!

Midnight: Just had a peek of the plans for the next operation at Halmahera. As yet, I do not know exactly what part we will play. I do know that we will convoy one of the echelons with certain radio frequencies to maintain in the communication department. My responsibility, We leave tomorrow at 1500.

11 Sept 1944
At sea

Got underway with a group of LSTs for Maffin Bay and from there to our next objective in the Halmahera in the Molucco group of islands. We will also make landings of troops on Palau. In a speech by the Captain, he says that Palau will be most spectacular as there are strongly fortified Jap positions with some 40,000 Japs defending the island. No air opposition is expected, because the nearest Jap airfield is over 500 miles away. But at Halmahera is a different story. We will land our troops just 200 miles from 10 Jap serviceable bases. We can expect daily air attacks. We on the *O'Bannon* will go in on the first day, but the second day we will patrol the beachhead for the next two days. The Captain said the whole Pacific is on the move from the Northern Kriles to the waters of the Philippines. As editor of the Press News *Scuttlebutt*, I do keep up with the changes in the war geographically.

I expect we will be involved in a lot of action this trip. It seems that we have not done much to win the war but just be out here. I am getting what I wanted. If my number is up, it will be God's will.

12 Sept
At sea

Noon: Just left Maffin Bay with groups of LSTs and transports loaded with troops. I hope these boys are not overconfident. Anything can happen!

13 Sept 1944
At sea

We are still poking along with our convoy of LSTs, LCIs, transports, APDs. There are four destroyers. The *Lang*, my old ship, *O'Bannon*, *Nicholas*, and *Hopewell*, which makes convoy of some 45 or 50 ships.

There are five big troops transports in all. I went on the fantail today and soaked up some sun. Maybe got too much.

We all have our likes and dislikes when it comes to people, and I could never understand "brown nosing" in a situation like we are in. We are confined, or if you will, imprisoned on this little ship, and we have our duties cut out for us in detail, so what is one to gain by sucking up to the officers who cannot do what we do, nor can we do what they do. So, what is to be gained by brown nosing? Since we are so close, our likes and dislikes change too. We must get along! We cannot afford to make enemies here. Leave that for the Japs!

14 Sept 1944
At sea

It is midnight, and we are steaming along at 27 knots to investigate a target picked up by radar. Today we had a little scare, and we moved in closer to the convoy to bring our guns to bear in case of an air attack. Our radar picked up several aircraft. We don't know whether they are ours or the Japs. If it is the Japs, they will know where we are going and warn their Japs on the beach. I feel sure they know where we are going and will be ready for a fight.

15 Sept
At sea

Just heard some wonderful news: 173 Jap ships were sunk, and 50 Jap planes were destroyed, to make the largest victory of this war. (Where, I did not record.) We also received word that our troops landed at Halmahera (East Indonesia) unopposed. That sounds pretty good as we will be going in tomorrow morning. It will be a long GQ anyway.

One of the Crew, USS O'Bannon, World War II

16 Sept 1944
Morotai Island, Molucco Group (Dutch East Indies)

0730: We came in at sunrise for a little excitement. We were at our regular morning GQ, and about 45 minutes later, we were called to GQ again. A Jap plane sneaked through our air coverage and bombed a destroyer escort. Four of our fighters went after the Jap plane. The Jap shot down one of our fighters before they got him. I was listening to "fighter director" circuit on the radio. Our guys on deck saw the whole show. We went out to look for the pilot of the American plane, but there isn't much hope as his plane exploded when it hit the water.

1700: On watch now—went to GQ after the air scrap this morning as there were three more Jap planes spotted, but they did not come in for a fight.

The *Lang*, *Hopewell*, the frigate *El Paso*, and the *O'Bannon* are on patrol at a smart speed between Morotai and Halmahera, with no action to report.

Oh, yes! Today I saw my first active volcano.

1900: Good news! The *Hopewell*, the newest addition to the mighty DESDIV 21, shot down its first Jap plane when two attacked. The other Jap plane fled the scene.

17 Sept 1944
Patrol duty off Halmahera

Today being Sunday, all had intended to sleep late. Hoping to enjoy holiday routine. About 0600, ALL HANDS TO GENERAL QUARTERS!!!! A Jap plane dropped a "bomb" at our ship but missed. Rambo Murray was on the fantail and saw it happen. He said it was an auxiliary gas tank—it floated! The Officer of the Deck and our fire control officer, LT(j.g.) Huck, got criticized for not being alert???

20 Sept 1944
At sea

We are convoying LSTs to Aitape. More monotony. Would like to go into port and get mail. For the last three days, we have not been able to get any press news because the Japs have blocked the circuit. Still plodding along.

24 Sept 1944
Humboldt Bay

Returned to port at about 1800 after escorting the LSTs to Aitape—fueled the ship and had a movie. Last night, we had an unnerving experience. We almost smacked into a fully-loaded gasoline tanker, but we missed it by about 100 feet. Had we smacked it, there would be nothing left of this ship nor the tanker.

My mother sent me some pictures of herself, Norman, his wife, Josephine, and the kids. Made me bawl.

25 Sept 1944
At sea

0430: Left last night at about midnight to probably do some more LST convoying. Oh, well, life can be cruel.

26 Sept 1944
At sea

This my 5th Anniversary in the U. S. Navy.

We are on our way back to Morotai with a group of LSTs. Hopefully, this is our last trip of this kind. I have been staying out of the radio shack except for my watches, to copy the news press, and try to teach Carroll the Morse code. I am getting better acquainted with other members of the crew. Every division has a coffee pot where we meet to shoot the breeze.

One of the Crew, USS O'Bannon, World War II

28 Sept 1944
At sea

Nothing to report but the same old unpleasant monotony. We did have a change in our orders though; we are to escort a group of LSTs to Sansapor, on the northern coast of New Guinea. The Army Air Force should be commended for keeping the Jap planes off our necks. Our Navy guys must be doing a good job too.

29 Sept 1944
At sea

We should get in today and wait for the LSTs to unload, then escort a group of them to Sansapor along with the *Hopewell*. I am beginning to like this new executive officer. He is trying to please this temperamental crew. He asked Bowman to hook up the record turntable for music at certain hours of the day, which I had suggested to Bowman to do when I came aboard. His argument was that we can't have music in the radio shack—so in other words, to heck with the crew.

The Office of War Information predicted that the war would not end until two years after the defeat of Germany—and me with just one year to go.

30 September 1944
At sea

We arrived at Morotai this AM, and patrolled the beach until the LSTs unloaded—practically all day. Left again this evening; went to GQ at 1630. I was on watch at the time—stayed at GQ until midnight, which made a 12-hour watch. Two Jap planes flew over the beach. The Army shore batteries and the LSTs opened fire at once. It was more of a protection barrage than anything else. Of course, they were trying to hit those dudes. It is now 0400, and I have the watch 'til 0800, which is 16 hours on watch! Oh, well, that's life!

1 October 1944
At sea

Slept all day, got up in time to go on watch at evening chow. Rolling along at about nine knots. Due in Sansapor tomorrow morning. Learned through the news that Morotai had been raided by four Jap planes. One was shot down. Left the LSTs in Sansapor and picked up a medical team. In talking with a Pharmacist's Mate, he said he had made all the New Guinea invasions. He said there were only three casualties in the invasion at Morotai, and they were accidents. He said he had been out here 22 months and was on his way back to the States. We will begin tomorrow at sunset. Thanks to the Exec, we will get our mail as soon as possible. This guy really takes care of the crew.

3 October 1944
Humboldt Bay, Hollandia

This has been a hectic day. Boyte and I have received about 30 "Urgent" messages on the afternoon watch, and they are still coming in. There is something big going on somewhere. All messages are in code. We have ships of all descriptions here in port, but very few warships.

I am led to understand that we are to invade another island before invading the Philippines. The island is about 150 miles South of Mindanao. No mail waiting for us.

Learned the Urgent messages were regarding a DE, which was convoying a merchant ship and took a torpedo from a sub. It was being towed in a sinking condition. I suppose the Urgents were for us to pursue the sub.

I had a chance to swap duties to the Command Ship of Task Force 76. The ship is the *Henry T. Allen*. Maybe I should have taken it, but I prefer a ship that travels rather than remaining anchored.

7 October 1944
Humboldt Bay, Hollandia

These past few days have been pleasant with the Fox skeds secured; however, we have the "Dog" circuit going full blast. Once in a while, he sends a few messages. We have the record player in the radio shack to play at certain hours with music on the "V" Disks. Murphy tells us that the next operation will not be a pushover.

10 October 1944
Humboldt Bay

This loafing in port almost makes me feel guilty. The rest is doing us all good. We were in portable dry dock for 24 hours to straighten one of our screws.

(I have decided to eliminate some of the most boring info such as our boring existence on our ship when we talk about no girl friends and are generally shooting the breeze.)

12 October 1944
Humboldt Bay, Hollandia

Still here

14 October 1944
Humboldt Bay

We went out to sea for some antiaircraft firing practice. The shooting was very good, but the shooters received no praise from our Captain.

We came back in port about 1600 to find loaded transports and several more destroyers. The light cruiser *Nashville* is in port also. It looks like we are going to be busy. Artisani just came in all enthused over the "band" they have scraped together called the "The Joe Pot Jivers." While in dry dock, they (the Jivers) met a very good drummer and an accordianist off an LST that was tied up alongside the dry-dock. Last night, they got together on the

Solomon Islands, Dutch East Indies and New Guinea

foc's'le and, with no rehearsal, did a good job. They made arrangements to have a dance aboard an LST with 80 newly-arrived "WACS" as guests. Artisani is going to try and fix it for me to go along. Just what I need! Artisani struggles with his trumpet. His practicing gets a bit trying at times. (Nothing happened with the Dance.)

16 October 1944
Humboldt Bay

0400: On watch and awful sleepy. We got word at quarters yesterday to secure all unnecessary gear as the next operation will occur in rough seas. I will have to read up to find out where there is rough seas in this part of the world at this time of year. I thought our next objective would be Sangria which is located at the foot of Mindanao, I suppose the "Brass hats" may plan to strike a bit further up the line.

Someone brought a dog aboard as a mascot (mangy hound).

Went out for some antiaircraft firing today. Came back in and tied up with the *Taylor*. Artisanti went over to the beach to meet with the orchestra and set up the dance on the LST. It fell through. Only six WACS showed up. Some officer called the dance off. Jealousy???

We will be off to the war soon. The ships and landing craft are loaded to the gunwales with troops and supplies.

17 October 1944
Humboldt Bay

We leave at 0500 in the AM. We have a new radioman. His name is Zarnecki. He left the ship to attend radio school in Pearl Harbor some time ago. We can use him.

I don't think we will be in the first wave in the invasion. Maybe the 4th or 5th. We shall see.

CHAPTER 11

THE PHILIPPINE ISLANDS

18 October 1944
At sea—En route to Philippines

Our Captain gave us his usual speech about our next operation. We are surprised to learn that we will not be bringing up the rear after all. There are six escorts, the *Nicholas*, *O'Bannon*, *Taylor*, *Hopewell*, and two frigates, *San Pedro* and *El Paso*. We are to take this convoy of 68 ships right into the heart of the Philippines at Leyte, on Leyte Gulf. We may expect Jap PT boats, midget submarines, and air attacks day and night, and we will most likely have them.

Admiral Halsey reported by secret dispatch that all the ships that radio Tokyo reported sunk by the Japs had been salvaged and were retiring toward the enemy. The admiral is quite a card. If we don't get into this war up to our ears this time, we never will.

19 October 1944
At sea

0430: All is going smoothly. We go to GQ in a few minutes as a precautionary measure. We call it "morning alert." I am sure there will be plenty of air and sea protection around us as we proceed. Admiral Marc A. Mitscher is supposed to have about 80 carriers, and Halsey's Third Fleet should provide the protection we need. This must be the case, as four destroyers and two frigates escorting 68 ships aren't enough to do the job.

I think our Old Man likes to dream up more danger than there is as he did at Aitape and Morotai, which were a snap! The Philippines, I realize, will be a different situation. I think we will run into a heap of trouble. However, I feel that the "big boys" have taken care of the major opposition. We have enough ships and planes to subdue the Japs for a while anyway. Any kind of attack by the Japs will be on a small scale, in view of the plans and power dedicated to success.

2200: We are in calm waters now, but rough seas are expected. I feel sorry for the guys on the LSTs (floating bath tubs) and the transports—the guys who do not have the Sea Lubber's belly. Since we haven't been in any rough sea since I have been aboard this little ship, we will have a few sick lads also.

The Japs are really raising hell on our radio circuits. They have found our operational frequency and are driving us radiomen "nuts"!

These are quiet days on a calm sea except for the watches, drills, and reveille in the morning. The quiet before the storm???

20 October 1944
At sea

Nothing new to report. Standing watches, drills, getting a suntan, and sleep. General MacArthur[6] spoke on the radio, but there was a foul-up on the "net," and we didn't get to listen to him. Tomorrow will be a busy day. Report from Leyte says there was a one-plane attack that was shot down. Our Air Force guys are doing a helluva job. Halsey's Third Fleet was attacked by a large number of Jap planes, of which a large number were shot down by our planes and ships' AA (antiaircraft) fire.

Our Captain, over the speaker system, told us about Leyte. He said there were more than a million residents on the island with about 50,000 in one town and several towns with as many as 2,000 to 10,000 people in them. He went on to say that they are true American Filipinos. I hope so!

---

[6] General Douglas Arthur MacArthur, five-star American general (General of the Army)

One of the Crew, USS O'Bannon, World War II

We are passing about 30 miles from Palau, which the Marines took from the Japs about a month ago. One kid returned from the hospital and talked with a Marine that said the operation was worse for us than Saipan or Tarawa.

22 October 1944
At sea

We fueled at sea from a tanker that kept an old Navy tradition of sending over ice cream. What a treat! Our Captain did a super job of bringing the ship alongside the tanker.

We should arrive tomorrow or the next day. It doesn't look like we will be on the front line after all. One of our destroyers struck a mine that killed several of the crew, but don't know whether the ship was sunk or not. It seems that things are congenial here in the radio shack again.

Situations do change. Murphy came by for a nice visit. It seems that we won't get the bad weather as expected. If we do, this is the time of year for tornadoes.

24 October 1944
Leyte Gulf, Philippines

ACTION! CAMERA!

We arrived here in a cloud of smoke. I mean just that. All destroyers and destroyer escorts were making smoke to screen for the transports and tankers. So far, our boys have shot down one plane. The Japs sank one of the LCIs. There are Jap planes all around us. Obviously, the Jap planes are aiming for the big ships. There are five of our battlewagons here. The Old Man is stewing back and forth across the bridge, letting all hands know that he is in complete charge. We are at GQ and will be for the rest of the day. I had the mid-watch, and I am tired.

0930: Flash White—all clear. I did get an hour and a half sleep before we were called to GQ again. I don't know how many Jap planes came over nor how many were shot down. With all guns firing, they stayed for about an hour before we were secured. I went below and cleaned up, then relieved the watch, expecting another attack at any minute! Lousy reception on the Fox skeds. We are missing some numbers.

1740: Called to GQ again. I had just finished eating and went on deck. I saw a terrific antiaircraft barrage over the port beam, very close. Battleships, cruisers, and destroyers, including us, were banging away with all they had!

1945: Secured from GQ. The Japs torpedoed one of our ships. Don't know what their losses were as yet. We expect another attack in the middle of the night.

25 October 1944
Leyte Gulf, Philippines

0400: Quite a bit has happened during the night. All day yesterday we received Urgent reports that three Jap battleships, some cruisers, and destroyers were on the loose down by Mindanao, and our boys encountered them. From topside, we could see the flashes of gunfire and heard the rumble of big guns off in the distance. Hope we find out the dope (results) some time today.

Listening on the TBS now, we hear someone saying that he expects an air attack in 15 minutes, and his speed is 10 knots. Will maneuver by whistle turns. [I have forgotten what "whistle turns" are.]

Back to the battle yesterday, Bowman, whose battle station is on the bridge, said that he saw four of the Jap planes hit the sea. The way the LCI got sunk yesterday was because a Jap plane crashed on her (the beginning of Kamikaze attacks).

0700: Secured from GQ. I heard over one of our battle circuits about picking up enemy survivors. And someone requesting from some ship to make ammunition reports. When I relieved Miller, he said he heard over the battle circuit, "Have contacted the enemy and made several hits."

Don't know how much damage the Japs did in this morning's air attack. All ships laid a heavy smoke screen. We received a "Flash Blue" which means an air attack probable.

Oh! Oh! "Flash Red," under air attack! "Control Yellow," fire on any aircraft identified as enemy.

0915: Here we go to join CTG 77.2 (Command Task Group), under Rear Admiral Oglethorpe who is under attack and has been since 0720 this morning. The message said there were four Jap battleships, eight cruisers and many destroyers, which are split up in two groups. The Old Man was happy to receive the orders to join him. I will be too if we don't get sunk.

This morning as I was in the chow line with Miller, five Jap torpedo planes came in to attack the large ships. None were shot down as far as I know. The *Russell*, DD414, destroyer, crossed in front of a tanker that was firing and got sprayed with shrapnel from the tanker's shells. It is pretty exciting. Almost every destroyer has been ordered out to join in the battle. In our group, *Nicholas*, *O'Bannon*, *Lang* (my old ship) and another 1500 tin can are with us. Do hope we do some good.

1130: We have joined up with a large force: 5 battlewagons, 10 cruisers, and about 30 destroyers.
I am still shaking with excitement. We were called away to GQ, and when I hit topside, our guns and all the others were blazing away! The sky was covered with bursting shells. Gee! That's a helluva way to get awakened! One of our group is in trouble, and requesting immediate assistance. A force of cruisers getting the worst of the show.

1245: There were three Jap planes that came very close to us. Murphy came in to tell us that one of our planes had torpedoed one of their cruisers.

1830: We are still at it. The Captain gave us a little talk about the situation to date. Our Captain said there were two Jap forces, one from the North and one from the South. The North force attacked one of our carrier divisions commanded by Rear Admiral Sprague. He was my first executive officer on the *Ranger*, and Captain of the *Pokomoke*, which I put in commission. His force was attacked by three battleships, several cruisers, and several destroyers. Hits were made on all four of the carriers, but they will be ready for duty, except one. The Southern force got into it with our task force, and judging from a report from a Jap prisoner picked up at sea by the destroyer *Claxton*, in the same squadron with the *Beale*, two of the Jap battleships exploded, and five smaller ships were sunk.

The Captain said he did not know the details of the battle, but the Japs retired back into the San Bernardino Strait. He feels they will not be too much of a threat to us.

There have been air attacks all day long. Our five-inch guns have been blazing away. One of our destroyers is in sinking condition. Many Jap planes have been shot down. Oh, yes, the Captain said that there were no aircraftcarriers in either of the two Jap forces. He said the Japs are hard up for aircraft, which is obviously true, but the damage that one plane can do keeps us on our toes with modified GQs while this low overcast and weather permits.

A frigate got hit this morning by a Jap plane.

We are awfully busy here in the radio shack. Five of us are managing to handle six circuits. Three of them are always busy with coded messages and the other two are voice circuits. There is much excitement going on now. What's coming up next?

One of the Crew, USS O'Bannon, World War II

THIS SEGMENT IS WHAT WAR IS ALL ABOUT!

26 October 1944
Leyte Gulf Area

0335: Boy, O Boy! This old Lee boy is plenty tired. The other guys are also. We are still at GQ on a modified basis, which means that watertight integrity is in effect, and the water is turned off. I managed to get a bath during a "rest easy" period this afternoon. Modified GQ means four hours on and four hours off for the crew, but radiomen are on call all the time. The circuits must be manned.

There was antiaircraft fire over near the beach about 2000 hours last night. We are still under "Condition Red." Enemy aircraft are still all around us. I noticed that the personal animosities among us have eased. With our guns blazing away, and we bottled up in the radio shack, our guys are courteous and considerate. When the five-inch guns are firing, there isn't much tension, but when the 40mm start firing, and then the 20mm, we all feel that we are in deep do-do!

Now that we have joined the big task force, we have been hanging around the harbor mouth in an effort to protect the landing beach. It is a good thing that the Japs didn't catch all inside as they obviously planned. Guess today will be another busy day.

0405: I had hit the sack to get a wink or two of sleep 'til this came about. Our guns opened up on a plane with five-inch, 40mm and 20mm. As yet, I do not know the results.

This afternoon we picked up three of our airmen who had been in a life raft for 24 hours. They were very young guys. One said, "wait till I get at those Japs now." They were mighty glad to see us.

Two planes came over us for a strafing run; our gunfire scared them off. Both planes retired.

The Philippine Islands

This running to GQ every five minutes is getting to be a pain in the fanny. I was caught in the shower and had to go up with a towel around me. We did manage to shoot down a Jap torpedo plane. There were three Jap planes coming from the beach, two of them were on fire, and the third one met one of our five-inch shells and exploded. One of the planes on fire nearly hit us before crashing in the water. We learned from Combat (Combat Info Center) that 11 Jap planes had been destroyed.

We still have the three aviators aboard. I suppose the Old Man doesn't know what to do with them. One of the airmen said they left a Jap battleship dead in the water, but did not say why they wound up on the life raft.

With all my years in the Navy, I now know why all the training. Days are far from being dull!

Just noticed that I had forgotten to mention that a Jap plane dropped a bomb at us that exploded about 20 yards from us.

0845: We secured from GQ at 0600 this morning, and I picked up about 20 minutes sack time—no sleep. Went to chow and came up to relieve the watch until noon. Wasn't on watch an hour until called to GQ. A Jap bomber came very close to us heading for the transport ship area. We got off a few rounds at him but missed. The *Taylor* also missed. I am so tired that I don't give a damn what happens next; I just hope to get a few hours sleep before it does happen.

Our squadron is all alone again. Don't know what happened to the big task force. We are still under orders to keep patrolling the entrance to the harbor.

We were called away again about 20 minutes after the GQ. A low-flying Jap bomber was about 20,000 yards from us. One destroyer opened fire on it—missed. I wonder how long this will go on? I am getting code happy. A 12-hour watch with no relief.

1600: Still at GQ, and the air attack is still underway. The beach batteries are continually firing at the little bastards. Murphy said the Japs had made 13 consecutive air attacks. Just before we went to GQ, we were close to the beach, and we could see the Army artillery firing at the Japs positions on a hill. Don't know the results of the 13 air attacks, but will find out.

27 October 1944
Leyte Gulf

0035: Well, I can chalk up another hour or two of sleep with no air attacks. We have received several reports of a Jap fleet not more than 200 miles away in each report. One heavy cruiser and six destroyers.

The latest aircraft message reports that an enemy convoy is headed for the Philippines with troop reinforcements. I wonder if one of our admirals will try and take them on?

Many Jap planes have been shot down by our ships. Except in a couple instances, it is impossible to determine what ship got the credit for the kill. The P-38 pilots flew right into the bursting shells in pursuit of Jap planes on more than one occasion.

0245: Just talked with the coding officer. He tells me that we did not lose any ships in the surface battle. The Japs got the worst end of it.

We still have the air crew on board. They were shot down by gunfire from the Jap battleship. They landed within 150 yards of one of our ships, which ran off and left them. Twenty-four hours on a life raft is tough duty. They did have water on board.

I came up on deck to learn that a Jap plane dropped a bomb about 200 yards from us. Our 20mm crew said they made a few hits on the plane. The Jap planes are coming from a Jap battlewagon converted into an aircraft carrier, according to a coded message.

The Philippine Islands

1235: I am on watch again, and the Japs haven't given us any trouble. We went to GQ only twice this morning, for naught.

We unloaded our fliers on the Command Ship *Wasatch*. We have two crippled 2100-ton destroyers. The *Ross* backed into a mine and is standing deep in the water, and the other was hit by two shells from the Jap battleship as it was making a torpedo attack. Natives are coming alongside in their outrigger canoes. Our guys are throwing packages of cigarettes. All is calm and peaceful at present.

1630: Still calm and peaceful. The tin can that was shot by the Jap battleship is the *Grant*.
Well, well; we may not have too many air attacks in the future. Thirty P-38s flew in this afternoon, which should relieve the air-attack pressure.

1645: Right after I entered this past paragraph, we were called to GQ.

It is now 1915. I went out on deck and saw a Jap plane explode and make a suicide dive into one of our merchant ships. (We did not know that the suicide planes were called Kamikazes at that time.) Bomb explosions and gunfire are all up and down the beach. So far, the beach artillery has shot down two planes that we could see, and they were flamers. I wonder where the P-38s are?

28 Oct 1944

0430: All is calm and peaceful. I turned in last night at 1930 and slept till 0400 to go on watch. There were artillery fire flashes all up and down the beach. I do hope the Army is doing well. Last night during the air raid, a suicide plane made a dive on the *Louisville*, C-28, one of our heavy cruisers. The AA fire from the *Louisville* shot him down before he could do his job. Although he missed the ship barely, he came near enough to injure one man. The *Louisville* is anchored a short distance from our port quarter. The rest of the ships in the harbor started making smoke screens.

One of the Crew, USS O'Bannon, World War II

1830: We went to GQ at 1630. A P-38 was chasing a Jap plane, and a destroyer to the stern of us opened fire on both planes. The P-38s got away fast—so did the Jap. We've had nuisance bombings all day by single Jap planes. No damage was done.

Just read the press news. We lost a big carrier, two escort (Jeep) carriers, and a destroyer escort (DE). All sunk.
Had some shooting this evening at a lone Jap plane. The P-38s have the situation well in hand. They shot him down. About 20 B-17s flew over us today. It looks like the Japs will catch hell!

A dead Jap floated by our ship this evening. One of our whaleboats went out and got him. He had a knife wound over his ear and he was wearing only shorts. Hari-kari?

29 October 1944
Leyte Gulf

We got up early for GQ. Started to chow and was called away again. A P-38 shot down a plane near us. We are still at GQ. Our radar has picked up 36 Jap planes in three groups. Murphy tells us that Intelligence has advised that we will have a large attack today. The *Halford*, DD480, just came in without any torpedoes. I don't know where they used them yet.

The natives in their outrigger canoes are alongside swapping Japanese invasion currency for clothes. There are two very nice-looking young girls just sitting silently in the canoes as our guns are firing by radar since the skies are overcast.

[The *O'Bannon* joined Rear Admiral T. L. Sprague's Task Group 77.4 on 29 October 1944.]

30 October 1944
At sea

After several nuisance GQs, we got underway about 2200 to catch this carrier force. We left the harbor at 30 knots and hit some heavy seas. Some of our guys got sick. I almost did.

We arrived this morning. Boy, O Boy, this is a really mighty task force: 10 Carriers, 5 battleships, several cruisers, and scads of destroyers. I don't know where we will be looking for trouble.

Mr. Murphy read several congratulatory messages for the 7th fleet from General MacArthur, Admiral King[7], and Admiral Halsey, although they all read very much alike: wonderful, great…

We were going to pull into Palau for supplies, but apparently there are not enough to supply us. A few of the ships went in, but the rest of us are going to Manus Island for fuel and supplies. I guess we will be operating with the 3rd fleet, which is fine with me. I had rather cruise at 20 knots than 8 knots in an amphibious force.

The Captain gave us a talk to tell us about the action in the Philippines. Several ships were sunk—both ours and theirs. He also said he had received his orders to be relieved of command and would leave in about a month. This was good news for some of the crew.

1 November 1944
At sea

On our way to Manus. Received a message that our next skipper will be Alfred Pridmore, an Annapolis graduate of 1937. We hope he will have a sense of humor. He had only one other command, a four-stacker destroyer converted to what is known as a fast transport ship.

2 November 1944
At sea

Our Captain, in another of his talks on the speaker system, gave us some startling news. He said a Jap air attack at Leyte Gulf was made on only destroyers. Five tin cans were victims. One was sunk, two were victims of suicide dives; only one is back with the

---

[7] Admiral Ernest Joseph King – five-star admiral (Fleet Admiral)

fighting forces, but it is damaged. He also said that no Jap planes were shot down.

It is funny/strange that we miss out on the big shows, either we arrive late or arrive too soon! Probably God has a hand in the matter? I KNOW my mother is praying for me!

[The incident involving the *British Columbia Express*, which I am now writing about was published in *Sea Classics* magazine, written by Bud Feuer. I provided the story.]

7 November 1944
At sea

We got the job of escorting the LST to Hollandia anyway. Mr. Underhill told me that we have been assigned to join a task force of four battlewagons and several tin cans. He did not mention any carriers or cruisers. I suppose we will have good air protection around the Philippines.

9 November 1944
Hollandia, New Guinea

We are going to escort a transport ship to Leyte Gulf, and meet with the rest of our squadron there. My old ship, the *William D. Porter*, is here. We left it in Manus, but with us rolling along at 10 knots, it must have passed us. I shot the breeze with Lee on the light, and he was coming over for a visit, but we had to fuel and that took too much of the day. We leave about 0500. LT(j.g.) Bonn, on the "Willie Dee" sent over his regards. Nice guy!

10 November 1944
At sea

We were at sea early and met the *British Columbia Express* to escort to Leyte. It is a Norwegian-manned ship with a large group of MacArthur's staff aboard. Our Captain was going to send an officer and radioman over but decided on a signalman instead. He was afraid he would not get the radioman and officer back aboard.

Joe Hudson, the signalman, got the job. This will probably be our Captain's last trip, but who knows? Yep, he received his orders yesterday, in detail.

COMDESDIV 21 sent an urgent message that they were attacking a Jap sub and gave us the position and amplifying the report later.

14 November 1944
Leyte, San Pedro Bay

So much has happened that I cannot remember it all. Yesterday afternoon, we were in the mess hall enjoying a movie. Called to GQ. We tore madly out of there with our guns blazing away. I arrived at the radio shack to find Murphy (LT) scared and nervous trying to encode an Urgent message. He was too nervous to encode it, so he said to send it out plain language. All our guns were raising hell at this point. I was on the Fox skeds typing a long message at the time, and I can truthfully say that I was not scared. Somehow, I felt that God would take care of us. That faith is still with me. The message, of course, was a call for help. Honaker was trying to break in on the Commander Task Force circuit, and Butler was on 355 KC, while I was trying to goose all the power I could from the transmitters. Jap planes were attacking us. One of our 40mm crews shot one down. The Captain proved to be a competent man. He maneuvered the ship close to the transport, which placed us between the transport and the oncoming planes. It caused the transport to have an umbrella of fire over the ship. The Jap planes dropped bombs, but, Thank God, all missed. Our guys on the guns were really getting rid of a lot of ammunition.

While in the radio shack, Butler, Miller, and Honaker were pale around the gills. Butler told me later, also Mr. Murphy, that it was the first time that he was scared. Miller made a mad dash for his life jacket—which he always carries wherever he goes and keeps it by his chair when he is on watch. Today he put it on. Butler was on 355 KC calling Leyte. Honaker finally got through on the task force circuit with the Urgent message. By this time, the planes had been driven away, and they didn't come back, but they did attack the convoy about 20 miles ahead of us. We got in port this morning and when we were passing near the transport, there were a group of guys on the bow that gave us a rousing cheer! (It was reported that our Captain was awarded the Legion of Merit, and in my view, he deserved it.)

In reviewing the action, talking to the guys who were topside to see all that was happening, a ship on our port side shot down one of the planes that crashed very close to the *British Columbia Express*, and a P-38 shot down another. One of the pointers on one of the 40mm guns fired 300 rounds of ammunition without getting a "commence firing" order. Neither did he have a target!

Hudson, who made the trip on the transport, came back with a Norwegian flag and pictures as souvenirs. He said they treated him like a king. He even had a stateroom! This has been an exciting time!

15 November
San Pedro Bay, Leyte, Philippine Islands

Went to a 5-minute GQ. Mistaken identity—one of our own planes. These P-38 pilots are really making heroes out of themselves. One in particular—Richard Bong is his name. He made a record of shooting down 26 planes in the European Theater. His score as of yesterday is 33 planes.

Dawn is drawing near, and I have the 4-to-8 watch. A lot can happen in the next hour or two. Naturally, an air attack is expected. The Japs never fail to send at least one plane in our direction.

I displeased "T.T." Murphy, a devout Catholic. He offered me and others Rosary beads. I laughed and told him only God can protect me; not beads. One of our group took the beads, and he isn't Catholic. I asked him if he got a prayer with them?

I learned why LT Murphy was so scared the other day when we were escorting the *British Columbia Express*. There were 50 planes

The Philippine Islands

in the attack! But 12 of our P-38s knocked down 26 of them before they could get to us.

Not much has happened since the first air attack the day we came in. All is calm and peaceful today. The natives came out in their outrigger canoes to exchange Jap invasion currency for clothes, soap, or anything the boys want to swap. I got a handful of Jap money for a couple of skivvy shirts.

We are at GQ now. Probably "Washing Machine Charley" (a Jap observation plane that shows up on our radar screen every day). Our night fighters are on the prowl too.

17 November 1944
San Pedro Bay, Leyte

We had an unrehearsed show on the foc's'le after chow this evening. Artisani made the whole show when he imitated the Captain as we bombarded the New Guinea Coast. The "Old Man" took it good-naturedly. He laughed until he cried. Just at the last of the show, we had an air attack on the beach. The Japs dropped a few bombs through a terrific umbrella of artillery fire. They caught one plane in a search light, and an LST shot it down in flames.

These air attacks have become a matter of routine. Everyone takes them in stride. The Japs always lose a plane or two, and in some case that is all the number of planes they send. It was a lousy day for flying. Rainy and cloudy, but the P-38s were up all day.

18 Nov 1944
Leyte, San Pedro Bay

This day started off with a bang! We went to GQ at 0600 for about an hour. While I was writing this, Bowman came into the radio shack white as a sheet, as the saying goes. He said the Jap planes were deliberately diving into our ships. We could be next. A P-38 had a Jap plane on fire, and it dove into a Liberty ship, which was burning like a torch. The plane must have been loaded with gasoline. The beach put up an awful barrage of fire, but bombs fell on those guys. All is quiet now. The whole show lasted what seemed like a few minutes. We should have enough P-38s up by now. I have become mighty fond of those P-38 guys. It seems funny how slowly the Jap bombers were moving over the beach. Five Jap planes were shot down.

1730: I had a sneaking hunch that those little Jap so-and-so's would come early today. We have been to GQ several times today. We fired on one of our own planes by mistake. It was a P-51 Mustang or Thunderbolt. It was a miracle that the guy escaped such a barrage.

Three Jap planes came out of a cloud and strafed positions on the beach. Three went in and three came out. They got away. Strange too, because we had plenty of our planes in the sky. We listen to the pilots talk on the radio.

I talked to a native today. He said the people are very happy to have the Americans back. He said that there is much singing and dancing in the province now. He kept us entertained and asked for magazines. He said the Japs were most cruel, took their food, etc.

19 Nov
San Pedro Bay, Leyte

The Japs came a little late today—a few minutes after reveille, three Jap planes came in with three P-38s on their tails. All three Jap planes made suicide dives at the merchant ships. All three missed but one, which hit the bow of one of the ships a glancing blow causing minor damage.

Eight were killed and 12 injured when one of the suicide planes hit a merchant ship. It was too far away for us to fire our guns, but close enough to see.

This has been a busy day. We topped it off with a 5-hour GQ this evening. The first part of it, a Jap "Sally" MTMB plane was over taking pictures, then more came over to strafe and bomb the beach. It was cloudy as the devil, so they may have gotten away. I am on the mid-watch now. (At this point, I write about the radio crew, my observations of these guys would not be of interest to you.)

20 Nov 1944
San Pedro Bay

Not much to report today. Had a short GQ this morning at 0645 that lasted about 45 minutes. The short ones add up. They get to be a pain in the fanny. All is quiet now, but, as they say, it is always quiet before the storm. Speaking of storms—we are expecting a typhoon. Rain is expected by the bucketfuls, and is raining now. It has kept the Jap planes grounded. Thank Heavens!

Over the radio, Tokyo is bragging about the suicide planes. They consider it "most honorable."

Could use some mail to cheer me up. They have a new FPO at Tacloban, Philippine Islands.

22 Nov 1944
San Pedro Bay, Leyte

It has been pretty peaceful for the past couple of days. Three Japs came over to take pictures, but no attacks. Our aircraft are all over the skies: four-engine bombers, P-38s and Mustangs. For the past few days, nine C-47 transport planes have been flying in and out on the airstrip on the beach. Our squadron has been assigned to the 7th fleet for temporary duty. The *Lang* is with us too.

Been getting a little sun these days. It's hot as blazes around here at day and fairly cool at night. That suits me.

The Captain came on the speaker sytsem to give us the results of the battle on 24th of October. Here are the enemy losses: Battleships taking part, 7; 2 were sunk. Carriers taking part, 4; 4 were sunk. Battleship carriers taking part, 2; 0 sunk. Cruisers, 14; 8 sunk. Destroyers taking part, 29; 9 sunk. The biggest part of the Jap retreating force was severely damaged. It won't take long if we keep on with these successes.

One of the Crew, USS O'Bannon, World War II

23 Nov 1944
At sea

0100: I am on the mid-watch. We went to sea this evening in a rush. We received an Urgent message on the way out. We are on a patrol duty in an effort to sink two Jap submarines reported in this area. It makes the "Old Man" feel pretty good to get back to sea. I am glad to be at sea also. One does not get much rest in the harbor, although there weren't as many air attacks. Out here, the Old Man is the boss, and he makes sure it is necessary before calling us to GQ. He is getting to be a decent old duck. Tomorrow is Thanksgiving, the "New Deal" Thanksgiving Day, and we hope to have the usual big meal with all the trimmings.

24 Nov
At sea

0400: They sent two minesweepers out as an immediate relief for us and the *Reid* (DD369). We were assigned to the Task Force that patrols the coast: 3 battleships, 2 heavy cruisers, 3 light cruisers and about 8 of us destroyers. The battleships are: *West Virginia, Pennsylvania,* and *Colorado*; two Heavy CL's: *Portland* and *Minneapolis*; 3 Light CL's: *St Louis, Cleveland,* and *Denver;* and DESDIV 21 including the *Lang, Reid* as part of DESDIV 21 .

There was a report from one of our planes that he had spotted TWO **GERMAN** CRUISERS????? Could it possibly be? Then we got another aircraft report of a cruiser and a destroyer. Our planes have control of the skies and everything else seems to be in control, even if temporary.

Our hopes of hitting a liberty port or the States in the very near future look mighty slim!

24 November 1944
At sea, late

I got those ships wrong in the first report. The BB's are: *Maryland, Colorado,* and *Pennsylvania*; cruisers: *Columbia, St. Louis,*

Minneapolis and *Denver*, and ten destroyers. This has been a most pleasant day. I spent most of the day sunbathing and admiring the beautiful scenery on the fantail. The sea is smooth; hardly a ripple, and the islands are glistening in the sunlight. A day for scenery lovers.

1930: The Captain gave us some more info on the speaker system. He said there were two alerts at San Pedro Bay. A merchant ship was struck on the bow with an aerial torpedo. Though not severely damaged, the ship had to be beached. The second attack was made by 25 or 30 Jap planes. He didn't give us the results of this attack, but added: "What do you think that many planes could do to two destroyers out here in the Gulf?"

We have been detached from the task force temporarily, and are on patrol duty off the coast of the Leyte Gulf. I like these patrols out here.

There are no nuisance GQs. We went to GQ twice today, one ending just a few minutes ago. "Bogies" were picked up our radar.

25 November 1944
Leyte Gulf, Patrol duty

Received the results of the 25- or 30-plane attack in San Pedro Bay and the beach. They did quite a bit of damage to the plane runway and got a merchant ship with a delayed action bomb. Our fighters shot down 21 planes. There is an air attack warning in San Pedro Bay right now.

We received orders to report again to the task force. This afternoon, no sooner had we gotten in position, than COMDESDIV 21 ordered us to report to the command ship in San Pedro Bay. We arrived late this evening.

Apparently our Captain isn't very well liked by the "Squad Dog," which is the reason for our little extra jobs. It made the Captain a bit peeved today. He sent a message to the CO saying, "First, you put me out in right field; now, you have put me out of the game." He gets a big bang out of his own humor.

Last night he "busted" a QM 3/C to Seaman in a fit of temper. Well anyway...We sailed into port under GQ and went over to the tanker for fuel. Then we secured from GQ. We finished and turned in. "Flash Red" was on the harbor again, but we didn't go to GQ. All ships were sending up a terrific barrage, and our ship joined in. Our "Condition Red" watches were still on the guns. The Old Man had to be sleepy also, or we would have been at GQ. We had fired quite a few rounds before "Flash White" happened at about 0100. I had the watch. It is 0300 right now. This is a screwy war—my first and only one!

Just finished reading Captain Donald J. MacDonald's reports on the *O'Bannon*'s actions before I came aboard. He was the previous Captain. Those boys had it rough, but I would have gladly swapped places with any of them!

26 November 1944
San Pedro Bay, Leyte

I believe we are to stay here for a while. Got mail aboard today, mostly Christmas packages.

The ships in the harbor knocked down two Jap planes in last night's raid. There were only three of them. One crashed near us, and the other crashed on the beach.

Late: I was in my bunk and had just got cool enough to sleep when I heard AA fire, but figured they would do the same as last night and not go to GQ, which is what the Captain intended to do, but one of the little Jap so-and-so's flew in very close and dropped bombs between us and an LST. That stirred the old man to call GQ.

Now that we are at GQ, all wide awake and alert, we have heard only a few rounds of AA fire—nothing more. Being as I had very little sleep last night, I am plenty tired, and I have the 4-to-8

The Philippine Islands

coming up. It is about 2300 now, and this looks like one of those long, drawn-out affairs. Damn this port anyway. We certainly aren't doing any good here. Here I am on the 4-to-8, plenty tired, and trying to keep Boyte awake. He gets sleepy and doesn't give a hoot what he types, whether it is right or not.

27 November 1944
At sea

Quite a bit has happened. We had an air attack about noon today. The *Ross*, the destroyer that had backed into a mine and was in a floating dry dock for repairs, was struck by a suicide plane. Don't know the damage. Later the *Ross* shot down another attacker before he could make his fatal plunge! This action here was to throw us off the scent, because the task force that we left a few days ago was attacked by dive bombers and torpedo planes with fighter escorts. The first wave was about 25 torpedo planes. The destroyer, *Mustin*, DD413, reported survivors in the water. We are anxiously awaiting the results.

We have been assigned to escort a convoy of 12 merchant ships and a few LSTs partially back toward Hollandia, 3-day cruise: two days out and one day to get back. There will be three destroyers: the *O'Bannon*, *Jenkins*, and *Cunningham*. A couple of DEs will be the convoy's only protection.

Things are popping, but it seems that we miss out on the big shows. Got mail today.

28 Nov 1944
At sea

Our Captain made a short talk saying DESDIV 22, patrolling on the west side of Leyte, sank a submarine.

Last night we were called to GQ at 0200. Then, after that, we had a "morning alert." Not much sleep. Then tonight, with the mid-watch coming up (midnight to 0400), I turned in early. I had been asleep about an hour—called to GQ! A sub contact, which lasted about an hour. I had a hard time getting back to sleep. Finally dropped off, then awakened for the watch. One powerful headache!

We were detached from the convoy and headed back to San Pedro Bay for some more air attacks.

29 November 1944
Entering San Pedro Bay

The Captain released the dope that in the task force air attack: Two ships were put temporarily out of commission. The *St. Louis* was hit by two suicide divers, and one smacked into the *Colorado*. Two barely missed the *Montpelier*. One disintegrated right above the ship. Several were killed and some wounded. The *West Virginia* just did avoid a "fish", aerial torpedo.

Seven new 2200-ton destroyers entered port today. All are the same size as the *O'Bannon,* except each of the four turrets have two five-inch guns, rather than one each, as we have on 2100-ton ships. These also have better protected 40mm and 20mm guns. Really are snappy-looking ships.

The Task Force that was hit is on our starboard bow.

1900: We went to GQ as we watched the task force at sea throwing up a terrible barrage. It wasn't effective enough because three suicide planes hit the *Aulick*, DD569, (I think that is the way its spelled), and they sent a tug out to get her. Another dropped a bomb on the bridge of the *Saufley*, DD465, badly damaging both.

The *Aulick* and the *Saufley* were patrolling the same station as us, and the *Reid* was patrolling, the other day when the Japs came in. God is really taking care of us, I believe.

Mr. Freetage just came in and said the *Culick* had been yelling for blood plasma all night.

The crew is quite disturbed; that makes five ships in three days counting the near bomb misses on the *Montpelier*, which damaged her hull slightly.

It seems these Army fliers are never where they are needed. As yet, they never have been but once when 50 planes came in. They seem to be burning up the skies all the time. All of us believe it would be best to get some Navy and Marine fliers over here instead of a lot of kids as they have in these Army planes. They should have a regular fighter patrol over all of our ships along the coast—but who am I to say.

There is wind of another landing coming, and indications or scuttlebutt says we are going to be right in on the first wave. This one is supposed to be right in the teeth of the Japs near Manila Bay. If it must be, it must be!

30 November 1944
San Pedro Bay

How time is flying—not by the day, but by the month. Got to see the *Aulick* today. It is anchored on our port quarter. Boy, is it a mess! The 40mm on the starboard side forward of the bridge has disappeared. Number two 5-inch gun is all fouled up. The bomb, which was on the plane when it crashed, penetrated the deck forward of the radio shack and exploded in the Ward Room. The other two planes that dove on her almost missed; both clipped the mast and did little damage. One was enough!

Also learned the *Maryland* was hit by a bomb. Killed 20 and injured about 30 guys. The *Saufley* had many casualties also, but both ships are maintaining their positions in the battle line.

I don't know why they are holding us here in the harbor—maybe for another stooge job. We have been very lucky so far. We always leave just before the Japs manage to get in a few punishing blows. God's will, I guess.

Our next operation will not be so rosy. The "brass hats" expect large losses in the Philippines, but they feel they can keep it to a minimum by keeping on the move. Where have I heard that before? Just hope we are not included in the "large losses."

2 December 1944
San Pedro Bay

Ah, me! Just 23 more shopping days before Christmas! The Japs have left us alone for the past couple of days because of rain. The sun is out now though, so we can expect some action soon. I think I know where our next operation will be—on the other side of Leyte, a place called Ormoc Bay. It seems to be costing us dearly to obtain control of this island. The most important thing that we are losing is human life.

3 December 1944
At sea

We just left the harbor to join a cruiser task force. There are the *O'Bannon*, *Nicholas*, *Halford*, *Lang*, *Fletcher*, *LaValette*, and the cruisers *Portland*, *Phoenix*, *Boise* and *Nashville*. There may be more than this. The Old Man has been wanting to get into some more action badly. I guess he feels that he needs the experience for his future command. I had expected him to be relieved long before now.

I went over to the *Wasatch* and *Mt. McKinley* for repeat messages. When I returned to the ship, there were two cute little native girls singing on the fantail for anything our guys would give them.

We were told that we are surrounded by Jap forces and given instructions as to what to do if captured.

4 December
At sea

Really whittling off those shopping days in short order. There is land on both sides of us, and we must be going through the Surigao

Strait. We are expecting the Captain to tell us where we are going and what we are supposed to do. There are four cruisers and eight destroyers in this force. I am sure we will be bombarding Jap positions on a beach somewhere. It has been a terrible day—lots of rain, but calm.

We seem to be cruising up and down in front of Leyte. Everyone is curious as to where we are eventually going.

Oh, yes, rumors are that one of the 2200 tin cans, which arrived here just six days ago, was sunk the other day.

5 December 1944
At sea

The rumor is correct. One of the new 2200-ton destroyers was sunk with just a few days of this war—nearly eight million bucks on the bottom of the sea. We are going into the bay where she was sunk tonight. We were told to get all the sleep possible because we would probably be up all night.
Another of our destroyers was "crash dived," or "suicided on," as Rambo Murray calls them, today. The *Mugford* by name.

The boys are breaking out ammunition and powder for tonight's action. We jumped to GQ three times this morning—all within 40 minutes! Oh, What Fun!

1700: Two Jap planes soared into the formation, obviously to attempt suicide dives. All hell broke loose! All ships opened fire, and both of them were shot down. They never had a chance!

During the excitement, Mr. Lewis, a little ensign, showed up in the radio shack to tell us that the TBS was out of order. He was so scared that he could hardly speak. Everyone else was scared too, I guess. There is such a thing as being scared and calm all at the same time.

The *Mugford* was hit again today and was lying dead in the water. We were assigned to tow her into San Pedro Bay, but somehow she managed to get her power back and is steaming along as smooth as glass.

6 December 1944
At sea

This is definitely "it"!!! Boyte, Carl, and Mr. Murphy took the coding machine and all Confidential and Secret publications over to the *Phoenix* to keep until we return—if we do!

As yet, there hasn't been any dope as to exactly where we are going released to us common folk. Only five destroyers will be involved. My belief is that we are going into Ormoc Bay—close in—to bombard Jap artillery and other Jap positions on the beach. I suppose we will write the necessary letters...

7 December 1944
At sea

We are returning from the all-night bombarding mission at Ormoc Bay, and I am tired as the devil! We steamed along at 30 knots until we got inside the Bay and formed a battle line. We fired star shells and opened fire. Personally, I could not see what we were firing worth shooting at. The Army let us know by flares where their battle line was. We went up and down the beach looking for targets and trying to draw fire. So far, a piece of cake. Everything went along fine until the Jap planes came over. For a while during the bombardment, a big old beautiful moon came up behind us. What a target! No return fire. This is one lucky ship!

The planes came over; we put up a pretty terrible barrage, so we didn't have much trouble.

Right now, I could sleep for a month. Today is the "Pearl Harbor Anniversary." Wonder what is in store for us?

The Philippine Islands

There is scuttlebutt going around that 125 planes attacked the cruisers right after we left yesterday. We'll see how true it is.

At first, I was going to write a detailed description of all the action I've seen but now it all seems so unimportant.

Should be in San Pedro Bay shortly.

1200: We joined the four cruisers outside the bay. Coming into port now.

Midnight: It is true that ignorance is bliss. Last night we missed the Jap task force by about 30 minutes. That was the meaning of all the Urgents to COMDESDIV 21. We had orders to intercept them. Three Jap destroyers and two cruisers were spotted but somehow we missed them.

The cruisers were unharmed after the air attack the other day, but three destroyers weren't. The Mahan was sunk by a suicide crash. It's one of the new 2200-ton destroyers. The Cooper is the name of the one that was sunk the other day. Two were seriously damaged when the Mahan got it. Seems like the *O'Bannon* just misses everything. It is a lucky ship.

8 December 1944
San Pedro Bay

0100: Received orders to get underway for fuel. We will probably leave early in the morning. Mr. Haynes told me that we were going out to join a task force, and there will be several ships moving out. So, there must be something up.

This is a helluva life! A guy never knows what tomorrow brings. When we leave anywhere, there is a possibility that we won't come back. It has been one year now since I have gone on liberty. It sure is lonesome with no women around!

We couldn't come alongside the "Limey" tanker last night. There was no way to communicate with it. The Old Man sent a message to them this morning which says: "Tried to raise you last night by light, radio, and megaphone at 300 yards, and I am coming alongside." Those guys weren't losing any sleep.

We took on fuel and ammunition and are now unloading empty shell cases onto a LST which is alongside. The *Hopewell* called on the TBS to tell us that she had mail for us and the *Nicholas*.

1430: Just transferred our Confidential publications and coding machine to the cruiser. Looks like we are going on another shot at Ormoc Bay. Since we will be going through Surigao Strait, the old guys on board call it "Slot Duty" as they recall their days steaming up "The Slot" in the Solomon Islands.

There is tension, excitement, a few touches of fear, mixed along with fatigue, when we go on a mission, and then there are sighs of relief, which describes our feelings on this kind of duty.

Learned that we will stay up there all day tomorrow as there are 14 LCIs loaded with troops for a landing. We are advised to get as much sleep as possible. No one needs the advice. We will be going to GQ at midnight tonight. We are to expect aircraft and surface craft at any time. We will have air coverage from dawn to dusk by the Army Air Force.

9 December 1944
At sea

We unloaded the soldiers without mishap, and we are now on our way "home." Went to GQ at midnight, and Butler and I went out on deck to try and sleep 'til 0400, then take over the watch so the others could sleep. We had blankets and life jackets but it started raining. We couldn't sleep, so we took over the watch until 0800. Then we had a corned beef sandwich and coffee.

The Army was supposed to provide air coverage, but no planes showed up. The Army said the airfield was so covered with water that they could not take off.

It is now 1100. I hope they come soon. Weather is clearing, so we could expect a Jap air attack at anytime.

1730: We secured at 1100. I went below, took a shower and hit the sack and died! If I didn't have to go on watch, I would be sleeping yet.

Yep—everything went off better than "according to plan." We can thank the Lord for the lousy weather and everything else that fell in our favor.

1800: We are rounding the southern tip of Leyte now. We got through Surigao Strait and should be in about 2200.

10 December 1944
San Pedro Bay

Here we are; Sunday morning and I am on watch. We arrived about midnight. The *O'Bannon* and *Hopewell* were assigned to CTG 78.3 (Commander Task Group) for duty. This Commander usually keeps us at anchor for a few days, then assigns us odd jobs, such as patrol duty, or some convoy out a hundred miles or so, then back in port.

Broke an Urgent message just now. The *Hughes*, one of the new 2200 destroyers, got it tonight—a bomb and a suicide dive bomber. Seven killed, one missing, and fifteen injured. Flooded fire rooms and engine room, and, of course, no power. That makes five of the seven 2200 tin cans that came out here about a week ago. If this one sinks, it will make three, and the other two were seriously damaged. All five by suicide planes. It's a miracle that we have survived, but I don't want to speak too soon. We could get ours in the next few minutes. The 2200s look more formidable to a suicide diver!

One of the Crew, USS O'Bannon, World War II

We went to GQ this morning early, after which I sacked out until 8 o'clock.

The Captains of the *O'Bannon, Fletcher, Pringle, Stanley Stevens, Dashiell, Phillip, Paul Hamilton, Hopewell, Howorth, Shaw, Moale, Allen Summer, Laffey, Walker, Barton, O'Brien, Ingraham, and the Lowrey* are all meeting on the *Nashville* being briefed on the next operation, which means we will be right in there in the first wave this time. Personally, I am glad. Maybe I won't be later.

A funny thing happened over on the *Fletcher, DD445:* 25 MEN MUTINIED! They had meetings in the mess hall and made up a list of what they demanded, such as: Less "slot duty," more liberty, better chow, etc. Fifteen men are to get General Court-Martialed. Don't know what they will do with the other guys. They are Nuts! Maybe they feel they will be on safer ground? (I believe they made a movie about this several years ago?)

12 December 1944
At sea

This morning, Murphy and I took all of our Secret and Confidential publications over to Tacloban. It rained all the way, and we waded in mud and finally found the publications issuing office. No one could tell us where it was.

We are on our way, with landing craft all over the sea and on the horizon. We are supposed to protect them! Our Captain told us where we are going. It is Mindoro, just as I had figured. We will be at sea two days and three nights. The Captain said the landing will be a "pushover," but the trip up there and back won't be. We must be on the alert for the "fanatical people" who have it in their minds to stop us at all costs. He said that the battleships and cruisers that stopped the Japanese on the 25th and 26th of October will be our protection, with the aid of four "baby" carriers, together with Halsey's Third Fleet, to stop all Jap ships from coming down out of "Empire" waters. The Captain said he did not want to alarm us, or put fear in us, but he must make us realize the importance of keeping alert.

The Captain also said that on "D Day" at Mindoro, the *O'Bannon*, *Fletcher*, and *Hopewell* will be assigned to bombard the beach as we did at Aitape. He said he intended to put our ship as close to the beach as possible.

There is a concentration of about 1000 Jap troops in the area very near where we are to land. We are supposed to receive help from Philippine guerillas, as they will know where the landing is to take place.

The Captain said that we hold most of Leyte, half of Samara, and practically all of Mindanao, outside of the larger towns, because the Philippine guerillas are with us 100%. He added that Luzon is considered the enemy territory.

To Mindoro, which is less than 100 miles from Manila, we go through the Surigao Strait and straight up through the Sulu Sea. (The Sulu Sea is situated between Borneo, Palawan and the Philippines.)

13 December 1944
At sea

Dawn finds us plodding along slowly. Eight cruisers just joined us. We learned that another destroyer was sunk night before last. They are picking on the destroyer Navy.

We have been hopping to GQ all day. Just as we secured, just before dusk—around 1700 hours, a suicide plane flew right over the fantail, where I was getting a haircut. The sea was as smooth as glass. He made his fatal dive on the *Nashville*, about 1600 yards away, with two bombs exploding while the guys on board were lined up for chow. A huge fire is raging on the ship, and her small ammo is exploding. [I later learned that the admiral and captain were killed by this attack.]

A few moments ago, a group of Jap planes flew over the surrounding hills right through our air patrol on this side of the

One of the Crew, USS O'Bannon, World War II

convoy, and all destroyers opened fire with everything they had. It changed their minds, and they flew back. I do hope the Marine air patrol got them. While we were depending on the Army for air coverage, our guys were singing that new song, "Come out, Come out, wherever you are." These Marine pilots are a legit bunch. They stay in the air as much as possible, while the Army is afraid of getting their feet wet in a little bad weather.

The fire is under control over on the *Nashville*. We don't have a casualty report yet. I don't think we will get much sleep from now on.

We have a 2nd LT on board, who used to be a cameraman for Paramount Pictures, to report the action. He seems to be a nice guy.

I will have to catch up on the happenings for the past few hours since the *Nashville* was attacked. A Jap plane came up over the horizon and a destroyer on our starboard quarter opened fire, long range, and got him! We got in a few salvos at another suicide diver trying to do his thing. A P-38 dove down into a barrage of fire and knocked the Jap plane down in flames. It landed very close to an LCI loaded with troops.

1900: A few minutes ago, I saw a beautiful sight. A cruiser started to barrage at a plane I could not see. Obviously, the cruiser was firing by radar, then all ships opened fire. As it was almost dark, it was a pretty sight to see the tracer fire.

I wrote "A cruiser" in the above paragraph: It was the *Nashville*! Beautiful!!

[*O'Bannon* joined Admiral A. D. Struble's Task Group 78.3 on 12 December 1945.]

14 December 1944
At sea

On the mid-watch (12 midnight to 0400. I do my writing while on watch). Butler and I did manage to get a shower last night. The Captain made a short talk telling the crew that in order to have the ship on its toes tomorrow, he was going to put the ship on a condition watch, but keep "Condition Able" set (all doors and hatches dogged down and ventilation closed off). He allowed all hands to go below and get bedding. Now it looks like the ship is loaded with dead men all over the topside. The old boy is pretty considerate when it comes to sleep and GQ. I appreciate it. The tempo will move a bit faster starting about dawn. Those fanatical little sons of Heaven are to stop us or die trying. We intend to help them die!

Whatever could prompt a man with just an average intelligence to take his own life and kill other men as that Jap did yesterday? What is behind it? What compels him to do it? Does he fear for what we might do to his family and loved ones? How could a man like that love anyone? He has to love his country more than anyone or anything on earth.

Oh, yes! Last night a beautiful barrage knocked down a "crash diver." He went into his dive and never came out of it. He wasn't in flames, but I do not see how anything could penetrate that barrage of fire power!

We went to GQ at 0550 this morning, and it is now noon. We have the ship "bottled up" below deck, except for the mess hall. Butler and I took our blankets out on deck for a little rest until chow tonight. I haven't seen any enemy aircraft today, nor have I seen any of ours. The report is that our planes had a field day yesterday knocking down Jap planes.

We are on the open sea now, so I don't expect any air action until this afternoon. The Captain intends to keep us at GQ until day after tomorrow night. Man, O Man! That is a long time to live in this sweat box!

The *Nashville* lost 27 men yesterday, and she turned around and went back. [Later I learned that the *Nashville* lost 173 men including the admiral in charge of the operation.]

15 December 1944
Still at Sea

On 4-to-8 AM watch. We stayed at GQ all day yesterday—needlessly—as there were no Jap aircraft on the scene. Our Captain secured us when it got dark about 1900. I borrowed a piece of canvas and slept on deck from about 1900 'til 0330. Except for being a bit stiff from the hard surface, I feel pretty well rested.

I suppose we will go to GQ in about an hour as today is "Dog Day." "H" hour is at 0720. We have a bombardment coming up, but something tells me the Japs will be ready for us. A "pushover" the Captain said, which I question.

Well, well! Two destroyers got a surface contact, and proceeded to sink it with shell fire. We watched them get it in a cross fire on the horizon, and a duel ensued. Soon there was a large explosion, and it is still burning. There were several more contacts. The *Laffey* got one—don't know the outcome. It won't be long now before we start bombarding. It is still dark. One of our ships is under air attack.

Man, O man! Two suicide planes came in and struck a cruiser and two LSTs. It's awful to see one of those things come down, and when they hit a ship, there is a flaming explosion. They take a large number of lives. It is reported that the *Nashville* lost 147 men killed and about 100 injured.

A report just came in. Bowman said only one LST was struck by a suicide plane, but it looked like three of them got hit. The planes were on fire when they hit the water.

The Philippine Islands

Astern of us, two of our destroyers sank a Jap destroyer, we think. Whatever it is, it is burning furiously! The report came it that they have contacted another Jap destroyer. It is close, because the report came in over the TBS. Five suicide planes came in, but only one hit. Still makes a guy a bit nervous.

I went outside and saw two ships burning. The LST is in one big cloud of smoke. The other ship seems to be smaller than the LST.

We have contact with four ships moving slowly. The *Boise* was ordered to go out with a destroyer. Maybe it will be the *O'Bannon*.

The LST was 738. All Navy personnel were rescued. It had soldiers aboard, but do not know how many were killed. There was just one big explosion. The destroyer alongside was slightly damaged and is picking up survivors.

Here we are on the *O'Bannon* sitting around like we are in a San Francisco bar. How can it be? The fire is out of control on the LST, and the destroyer that was taking on survivors alongside is pulling away. This report was on the TBS. The destroyer that went alongside the LST had 15 men injured and one missing when the LST exploded. I was talking to Lyons, one of our torpedomen, who said he saw chunks of metal flying through the air. Both ships are still burning.

Two suicide planes dove on the *Howorth*, formerly a tin can in our squadron. One knocked off the SC radar antennae, and one missed. Close Call! What disgusted me is that while we were bombarding, a herd of cows ran out of the brush, and we let them have two salvos right in the middle of them. The Captain told the "boss" that the cows were in his target area. The "boss" said fire away; where there are cows, there are people, so, a few unfortunate souls paid the price.

Today about 1530, a single Jap plane flew over us when all hands, or at least a few of us, were trying to get some sleep. The ships opened fire, but he flew away unharmed.

One of the Crew, USS O'Bannon, World War II

[NO MOVIE CAN PORTRAY A WAR LIKE WWII. ONE COULD NOT BE MADE LONG ENOUGH, AND THEY WOULD NEVER PORTRAY THE BOREDOM IN MANY INSTANCES. WHY WOULD ANYONE IN HIS RIGHT MIND HOPE FOR 'ACTION' TO RELIEVE THE BOREDOM?]

1955: A few minutes ago all ships, and guns on the beach test-fired. Being inside, I didn't see it, but they tell me it was a beautiful sight. Then the Japs came. A few guys on topside said they saw firing and a few explosions. Could not tell. Could not see the results.

This is a screwy war! Most of the time, a guy is in a box seat feeling sorry for the guys under attack, then a cold finger runs up his back when he realizes the attack could be on him.

2055: All is quiet now, and we are on our way back to Leyte. I feel rather tired of it all now that the excitement has subsided. We have secured GQ, but I cannot go below and hit the sack because I have the watch until midnight. Did not get any sleep, but did have a shower, as we had a break in "Condition Able." The room was full of broken light bulbs, so circuits were shorted due to the firing. The need for a shower overcame my fear of cut feet. I have another boil on my forehead. Haven't had too much time to think of home and my girl friend, as my mind was too busy elsewhere.

An LST carries 150 men and 16 officers. On one that was sunk, only thirty members of the crew were saved, and 90 were saved on the other. Both were full of soldiers and equipment. One hundred forty-seven were saved on one, and I don't know how many were saved on the other one. "War is Hell." I hate to think of the families back home waiting for those guys. Makes me realize I have a heart, after all.

16 Dec 1944
At sea

We secured from GQ "morning alert." Hope it stays that way until we get in. The weather is rainy, which may keep the Jap planes down.

I forgot to mention that the *Fletcher*, *Hopewell*, and *LaVallette* were the first ships to bombard the beach, which is no feather in our cap.

Mr. Haynes (son of a Nashville, TN, judge), gave me the dope of about the next two weeks. We will have only one day off patrol duty, which is Christmas Day, then we will patrol back and forth to Mindoro. Mr. Murphy said that we have not been assigned to the next operation coming up in about two weeks, but there is a possibility that we will be assigned. I hope we are.

17 Dec 1944
At sea

We jumped to GQ a couple of times today, but they were friendly planes. When we pick them up on radar, some of our planes do not turn on their identification apparatus, which causes us to hop to GQ.

As a precaution, to prevent a suicide plane from taking a heavy toll, our Exec, Mr. Wiss, has suspended the chow line and asked the crew not to gather in large groups. The chow line is feeding only 20 men at the time. This evening, ten officers gathered on the main deck. Ha! The "brains" are setting good examples. We hope to be in tomorrow, and we all are expecting mail. We start patrolling Surigao Strait some time today—where the *Nashville* got hit.

1515: We hopped to GQ about three times today. Once, three Jap planes came in view. One of them gave us some target practice. He flew about 200 feet above the water. I came inside when we started firing. The *Hogan*, another 2100-ton tin can, was blasting away and not even coming close. Before I came in, I saw a couple of shells land just beneath the plane. Learned later, on the TBS, that the *Hogan* shot the plane down. As I said before, this is one helluva war. Most of the time you have a box seat with the action around you, like in the movies. The other two planes did not come in.

A couple of days ago, the doctor performed an appendectomy on a young guy. He is okay today. I have another boil coming on my proboscis—painful as hell.

18 December 1944
Entering San Pedro Harbor

We were at GQ for an hour-and-and-a-half last night at 1800 and fired a few rounds at snooping Jap planes. They did not come in to attack. It is just the suicide planes that have no respect for our guns. They don't live long anyway.

Correction: I made the statement that the *Hogan* shot down that plane yesterday. One of our fighter pilots did the job. We have good air protection this time.

The boil on my fanny is really sore. I have to sit on one cheek. Rambo Murray has two of them. One on his neck and another on his forearm. Why are we the only victims? Mail today, I hope.

19 Dec 1944
San Pedro Bay

We missed out a convoy to Mindoro. We will be on our way there in a couple of days. Waiting for my Christmas packages, and my usual bourbon-loaded fruitcake from my mother.

Later: Sometimes I wonder just exactly what wisdom is—who are the wise ones? One could never tell by the literature they have on the market these days. After reading so many stupid articles about the war as it is, and knowing how wrong the authors are, a fellow begins to wonder if these people have been pulling the wool over our eyes always? Sometimes, I want to say, to hell with it all and remain as stupid as I am always. What I know won't do me a helluva lot of good, unless I want to write a history book, which I don't! What am I fitted for in this world in the future? In the Navy, I am considered to be a fairly savvy guy—but that's in the Navy!

21 December 1944
San Pedro Bay

Last night a funny thing happened, and yet it would not be so humorous if things had turned out differently. I was in my bunk, and we were called to GQ. Before I could put on my pants, our machinegun batteries had opened fire. I got up to the radio shack, and found Bowman crouched in the corner of the passageway. The door to the superdeck was jerking with every blast of gun fire. I bumped into him, then noticed the door, and went out and closed it. The door is easily sprung under that kind of punishment. I think my old buddy, Bowman, dreams about those suicide bombers too often. We all do! Anyway, the plane was shot down by the ships in the harbor. It was a big twin-engine job on what is believed to be an observation patrol. We secured GQ, but it was called again a short time thereafter. Then secured again.

Well, well. Miller received his orders for a transfer back to the States for new construction. It is well that he goes. The guy lived in mortal fear all the time.

1930: Went to GQ and remained for about an hour and fifteen minutes. The radar picked up "bogies" in the area. We didn't do any firing as we did the night before. Due to the heavy barrage being rained so low, the *Radford* took six 40mm of our shells in the bow, and the *Dashiell* had to go in dry dock for minor repairs—Friendly Fire! The plane that caused this did not get away.

Got a sweet card from my Mother, who thinks I am "sick at heart and need a haven of rest." I don't feel that weak-kneed yet.

One of the Crew, USS O'Bannon, World War II

22 December 1944
San Pedro Bay

This has been a lazy day. I had the morning watch and slept most of the afternoon. Leyte now has a radio station, and we have picked up some swell programs: Morton Gould, Fred Waring, and others. We will have to keep tuned in. They also have a program called "The Voice of Freedom" transmitted for the benefit of the people of the Philippines. It is filled with new comments about the war progress. We need that too!

We had an air-raid alert in the middle of a good musical program, which went off the air as we went to GQ.

We must have lost a fighter during the raid. There was no damage caused by the raid. The fighter pilot came on the circuit to tell that he was chasing three bogies. Then we lost contact. We assume the Japs won the chase.

23 December 1944
San Pedro Bay

This day has been quiet and easy. We got a lot of mail.

24 December 1944
San Pedro Bay, Leyte

Christmas Eve and a quiet day here in port. Chuck Marshall is my assistant with the files (a collection of ALNAVs and other 'must keep' documents). We went to GQ this evening for about 15 minutes. Four bombs were dropped on the other side of the *Fletcher*, and one Jap plane was shot down. Now that the moon is up, we can expect more Jap attacks. I went to the head a few minutes ago, and the beach is sending up a beautiful barrage. It made a beautiful Christmas fireworks, but not for the guys on the beach. They were serious. "Flash Red" is still on, and the Jap planes are still in the sky, but we are not at GQ.

We have a Christmas tree, which is kind of withered, mounted on the bow of the ship, but we do have the Christmas spirit. At chow, every man received the name of another sailor. The Exec's idea. He has to write him a Christmas greeting. This Exec is Jewish and a swell guy, and he is enjoying watching the crew celebrate Christmas in every way possible.

Our new Captain is now aboard. A giant of a fellow, and he has not relieved the "Old Man" yet. I think I have the dope on the next operation: it is on the island of Luzon at Lingayen. We shall see...

25 December 1944
Christmas Day, San Pedro Bay, Leyte

This makes my 6th Christmas away from home. We have had a most pleasant day. I had the morning watch. At noon, we had a turkey with all the trimmings. I spent the afternoon listening to some beautiful Christmas music out on the superdeck, then went below to hit the sack.

About dusk, Jap planes came over. A gorgeous moon was up. They came to drop a few bombs on the airstrip. Night fighters intercepted them, and we could see the tracer fire. We were not called to GQ, but all hands were tense and alert. With Jap planes overhead, a fellow just cannot sleep, no matter how tired he is.

26 Dec 1944
At sea

1700: I knew the peace in port would not last too long. We received an Urgent message that an enemy battleship, a heavy cruiser, and six destroyers were headed toward Mindoro. We got underway so fast that we left one of our motor whaleboats on the beach. The "snipes" had one boiler taken apart for cleaning. So, we've three boilers instead of four. Hopefully, they have it fixed by now. The Captain was to be relieved by Lieutenant Commander Pridmore tomorrow. Both of them conducted a ship inspection and were to have a personnel inspection tomorrow with all the formalities of reading their orders, etc.

One of the Crew, USS O'Bannon, World War II

Holy Mackerel! Just broke down another Urgent aircraft encoded message that the Japs are getting much closer to Mindoro. We are about 250 miles apart. We have been underway about eight or nine hours now, and should be closing the gap. The Captain said we should expect contact by mid-morning. I am going to hate to see the old duck leave us—if he does—orders or no orders—this is serious, and I prefer to have him in charge.

Received another Urgent aircraft message that the Japs are shelling our positions on Mindoro. I wonder how Halsey's Fleet let them get through? Where is Halsey's Fleet? Everybody is asking that question. (I don't know where I got this info—"everybody.")

We have the *Boise*, *Phoenix*—the "boss" ship—both are light cruisers, *Minneapolis*, and *Louisville*—two old heavy cruisers—*O'Bannon*, *Hopewell*, *Radford*, and *Fletcher*. We also have four 2200 destroyers: *Barton*, *Sumner*, *O'Brien*, and *Lowry*. This is our force of 12 ships to intercept the Japs. They will probably run like hell before we get there.

We have a map of the Philippines by which we chart almost every enemy aircraft contact report of enemy vessels. I do hope we catch these bastards. I think we will give them a chase in the China Sea. That is, if they run. They are indeed an unpredictable bunch, so we must be careful not to run into a trap!

We had quite a few of our crew that were transferred before we left port, including Miller.

27 Dec 1944
At sea, at tip of Mindoro Island

Well, we steamed out of San Pedro from 25 to 27 knots and kept it up until a short while ago.

At 1100, we received an aircraft report. Our Army Air Force had sunk three of the Jap destroyers. One destroyer and a battleship were trailing oil and retreating at 25 knots, along with the cruiser

The Philippine Islands

and the other two destroyers. We pursued in the hope that the cripples would drop out of line and we could pick them off.

1700: Just a few moments ago, we picked up a Jap survivor. He had a funny little hat with an anchor symbol on it to show that he was a sailor. He was probably off one of the sunk destroyers. He kept saluting over and over again. The Exec made him put his hands over his head when he came aboard from the sea ladder. He smiled and winked and said "Me help." It caused quite a commotion aboard ship. There were enough rifles and pistols trained on him. The Exec didn't take any chances; he could have a bomb on him. We shall see what information he can give us. There is one thing for sure, this Jap isn't so fanatical that he would want to harm himself and others. He is in sick bay now to be treated for exposure, if any. Mr. Underhill, who understood some Japanese, questioned him, and was told that his ship had been torpedoed. Underhill said he had a "different dialect." They had the little guy so confused and scared that I don't think he knew what he was doing. He is a non-rated man and about 19 years old. We transferred him by breeches buoy to the *Louisville*.

Just received several aircraft reports that a battlewagon, a cruiser, several destroyers and transports were on their way to reinforce Mindoro only 225 miles away. We are going to run into some big trouble, 'shore as shootin'!

Our planes are giving us some good reports. We received orders at what depth to set our "tin fish." In a way, I hope that maybe this will be "IT". The sooner we will get to go home. There is scuttlebutt that we will go home in April, but we've heard that crap before. I don't see how anyone, including our admirals, can see that far ahead for any ship, but anything is possible.

I got relieved off watch for a few minutes and went back on the fantail to visit with Rambo Murray. Fires caused by the Jap bombardment were still burning on the beach. Two muffled explosions caused the guys sleeping on deck to sit up like they had been pricked by a needle. Goes to show that all hands' nerves are on an edge.

2150: Called to GQ. Don't know why yet. Probably some "bogies." It seems that the Task Force, or Task Group commander, on the *Phoenix* is trying to conserve fuel, as we are not going after the Jap ships. That all-day and all-night run at 25 or 30 knots didn't do our fuel supply any good. If we wait here off the beach, the Japs may try to come back and bombard again, then we will catch them. If we go after them, they may give us the slip, and we may run into a trap. There seems to be a battle of wits going on between our commanders and the Japs. Who am I to know? The Japs have us well spotted, and we have them well spotted. We have the larger force, but the Japs have a battlewagon, which can pick us off at a much longer range. Read the next chapter of "Famous Funnies."

28 December 1944
Patrolling of coast of Mindoro Island, Philippines

We were at GQ most of the night. While on a rest period, I saw a plane go down in flames. Don't know what caused it or whether it was ours or theirs.

An intelligence report stated that the Japs had made a beachhead on Mindoro Island, the night before last. Our Air Force sank four of the Jap transports and two destroyers, and damaged a battlewagon. As a result of the airmen's attack, fires were started on a Jap cruiser and a destroyer.

We are still patrolling up and down the beach. Fires caused by the Jap bombardment are still smoldering. The Japs must have done a good job.

The official news communique came out today telling the American public about our invasion of Mindoro. According to this news report, it was carelessness of the "Brass Hats," Admiral King and General MacArthur; the landing should never have taken place. To my knowledge, we don't have any news reporters out here, and I can't blame them. I am wondering how they can report such criticisms?

There will be plenty of times to celebrate Christmas after this war. We must keep it, this day, holy! We must be vigilant at all times to defeat such a fanatical enemy. We must beat him good!

We must expect enemy aircraft this evening. Something always happens when things are as peaceful as they are now.

2000: Something did happen, but it wasn't bad. We are on our way back to San Pedro at 25 knots, and we are maintaining that speed. We will probably fuel up and return to this area. The Jap fleet is definitely on the move. The last report was that they are about 450 miles away. A nice chance for our Liberators to make a call on them. I, personally, am anxious to meet the Japs and scrap it out. This war has to end sometime, and I am confident that we will be victorious!

30 Dec. 1944
San Pedro Bay

0600: We got in last evening, took on fuel and some food supplies; awaiting orders.

The Captain is going to present the Citation Bars and be relieved of his command by Captain Pridmore today. There will not be much formality. Our Captain is being transferred to command a destroyer division which is stationed at Palau, which means he will be out here indefinitely. I don't think the Old Boy minds a bit. He loves this kind of duty.

So far, I have not seen our new Captain smile. He is a stern-faced guy, and plenty big.

One of the Crew, USS O'Bannon, World War II

1 January 1945
San Pedro Bay

A nice way to start the New Year with the mid-watch. I have a splitting headache and a boil on the center of my back. Outside of that, I feel like a million!

Yep, I guess we will be home in March, according to the scuttlebutt, and it really seems to be true. It came from several sources, so it must be straight dope. I think I will take my dress blues out of my locker and scrub the stripes.

I hear the *O'Bannon* made the headlines in the States for repulsing the 12 Jap aircraft when escorting the *British Columbia Express* up from Hollandia.

2 January 1945
San Pedro Bay

We had a "happy hour" on the foc's'le. C division was on. (Communications Division) I played a Vallejo (Valley Joe) bartender. Artisani and Hoerger played the part of two sailors, and "Doke" played the part of a "bar fly." We dressed him up with three neckerchiefs and balloons for the bust. He really looked the part. All went off pretty good, but we should have pulled it off in pantomime as we started to do. It rained like the devil, but everybody, including the Captain, seemed hungry for some entertainment, so all sat right out in the rain.

I guess we will get underway tomorrow or the next day for the Luzon operation. I do hope we get back from this one as "stateside" is beckoning. I don't think we will be in the first wave of assault, but will probably be in the second wave. But of course, I DON'T KNOW!

2nd January 1945
Later in the day

Bowman and I took the two RAL radio receivers apart and cleaned them. I then took a sunbath on the fantail, then a shower and a short nap. As a reward for our performance in the "Happy Hour" yesterday, we took a whaleboat ride with three beers apiece, which made me very sleepy. We are preparing for our next operation and will leave soon. The battlewagons and cruisers left this afternoon.

3 Jan 1945
San Pedro Bay

The news about us going back to the States has spread like wild fire, even among the officers. The opinion is that DESDIV 21 and the cruiser division will be leaving for the States shortly. However, we do have another operation coming up that isn't going to be easy. Anything can happen. We will depart Leyte tomorrow about 1400 hours.

4 Jan 1945
San Pedro Bay

Talk about us going back to the States after this operation is the talk aboard this ship. Mr. Murphy feels that we are going also.
Our planes, B-24 Liberators, B-25s, P-38s, P-47s, P-51s and Corsairs, I think that covers all the aircraft except the transport planes, have been taking off all day to slap Jap positions. We will leave at 1400 hours. I don't think we will convoy any this trip as we radiomen haven't been getting instructions for drills and tactical maneuvers for the past few days. I do hope we don't run into any trouble. I think the best thing we can do is pray.

[The *O'Bannon* joined Rear Admiral R. S. Berkey's Close Covering Group, Task Force 77.3 on 4 January 1945.]

One of the Crew, USS O'Bannon, World War II

5 January 1945
At sea, AM

The Captain gave us the "hot dope," as he put it. He said our planes hit Formosa and Northern Luzon to soften them up for this invasion. Our battleships and cruisers have bombarded already. This force, consisting of four cruisers and eleven destroyers, is to protect the transports which are astern of us a few miles. We are clearing them a path. Not much opposition is expected, but there may be a "mess of Jap subs" waiting for us up the line. Also, maybe a few "dive smashers." This isn't going to be a pushover. We will know soon. Everybody is figuring on going to the States after this operation—Me Too!

At sea, PM

Today has been a busy day. We ran the Surigao Strait without mishap; and I didn't know we had been through it until this morning.

We were in sight of the transports in behind us. About 1500, we went to GQ. A Jap plane was snooping, which means we have been spotted. Then, we secured GQ. I was at my locker and had undressed to take a shower. Then, "All hands, man your battle stations," that sounded pretty urgent over the speaker system. I grabbed my clothes and steamed to topside to find the ship madly zigzagging. The *Taylor* had spotted a torpedo wake across the bow of the *Nicholas*. The *Nicholas* chased down the source. They rammed a midget submarine, and ruined the *Nick*'s sound gear. She then dropped a pattern of depth charges over the spot. Later, the *Nicholas* got another contact and said they were going to investigate. Have not heard the results yet.

Later we saw an abandoned C-47 over on the beach. It seemed to be in pretty good shape. More subs are expected as we proceed.

The Philippine Islands

6 January 1945
We are in the Sulu Sea

Nothing happened of interest today. We had a couple of sub scares and one air scare, which turned out to be one of our own.

Everyone is talking about going home on leave, and I am right in there with them. We will fuel at sea tomorrow and make the landing on the 9th. It is very choppy with some strong winds. We are moving at a slow speed, therefore, we are not bouncing all over.

7 January 1945
Sulu Sea

We must be getting close. A Jap twin-engine job flew over the formation this morning from a high altitude, dropped bombs and didn't hit anything. One of our fighters shot him down.
Sixty-four of our A-20 bombers and a group of fighter planes headed for Lingayen to soften the Japs up.

We fueled at sea today off a tanker. The transports are well in view behind us. There certainly are a lot of them. We have been hopping to GQ regularly, and I suppose we will be at GQ from now on.

Aha! I knew something had to happen today! About sunset, two Jap bombers came in. The *Boise* and one other destroyer shot one down from a good distance. Then, we started firing with our main battery. First the 5-inch guns, then the 40mm, and then the 20mm. We hit him good! Knocked a wing off, then it burst into flames. He fell between a cruiser and a destroyer.
We started picking up Bogies all over the skies, Some were our own planes. Just before the attack, one of our ships lost a man overboard. All the war ships were doing about 30 knots, and word came over the TBS, "Man overboard! Pick him up, if you can." After the attack, we circled to look for the guy, as did other ships—no luck.

One of the Crew, USS O'Bannon, World War II

We secured from GQ about 1930. I hit the deck for some sleep. "Condition Able" was in effect, so all hands had to sleep topside.

8 January 1945
At sea

I woke with our ship firing to beat the band. I thought maybe it was surface fire, but it turned out to be Jap planes again. Some of our night fighters are up, and we are making a smoke screen. A Jap destroyer came out of Manila Bay, and the destroyer behind us promptly sank it. More later.

During any of this action, it is easy to notice the fear on the faces of some of these men. Their faces seem to draw up in a strained expression. After "all clear" is sounded, they look wilted and tired. Some look like they have been bawling their eyes out; others look relieved, calm and complacent. Wonder how I look?

It is very easy for Jap planes to fly from China and Formosa, and there is a lot of Jap air power here in the Philippines.

Today has been a busy day, but I did manage to get some sleep until the evening meal though.

We went to GQ right after Chow. Oh, yes, I forgot to mention that we have joined another force with two of the "Kaiser's Coffin" (Jeep) carriers in it. It has a lot of bearing on what is to follow.

Five "Zeke" Jap dive bombers came in for an attack. One flew in a TERRIFIC barrage. How he got through, only God knows, and made a smash dive on the Jeep carrier *Kitkin Bay*. We could see it smoking later. Soon they took off all the personnel. Casualties are believed to be heavy. I think our own forces will torpedo the rest of the hulk. I am not sure. During the day, we came across a Jap life boat which had the letters "Maru" on its side. There were no survivors around it. We sank the boat with our 20mm guns.

The Captain seems to be a calm and collected sort of a fellow. Incidentally, he is from South Carolina. He is very cool under fire.

The Philippine Islands

We are due to land the troops in the morning. I don't think our task force will go in, but will patrol up and down in front of the Gulf. The *Boise*, with General MacArthur aboard, and the 1650-ton tin cans, *Edwards* and *Coughlin*, left us to go to the beachhead.

It is quite a sight to see all these ships open fire during an air attack. Something to remember for a long time to come.

We may expect all hell to break loose tomorrow. Maybe not in our direction, but over the troops landing. The Japs will probably send all aircraft available to the scene. One carrier lost will dent our air coverage somewhat.

9 January 1945
Still at Sea

I assume this morning's landings went off according to plan. The Japs knew we were coming, and according to the Press news, they said they were waiting for us, which is probably true. I do hope not too many guys got killed. We also heard by the news that Gen. MacArthur waded ashore, with the comment, "I have returned!"

This day has gone by with no mishap or excitement, surprisingly. We secured from "Condition Able," and I enjoyed a few hours in my bunk. That steel deck was beginning to tell on my old joints.

We have joined up with a force of three carriers and a couple of DE's. It is comforting to know that we have plenty of air coverage. Eight of our planes shot down a single Jap plane this morning. The poor Jap didn't have a chance.

I am not sure where the landing occurred, but suppose we will get the dope in tomorrow's Press News.

It seems that our chances of going to the States is getting even better, according to "T.T." He thinks we will go to a Navy Yard.
At 1800, we had a single plane attack. We threw up everything but the kitchen sink, but to no avail.

Because of the rough weather, the Task Force Commander recalled all of his planes. He didn't want any late landings in weather like this. The last four of our planes were landing when the Japs came in. We let go with everything we had, and they flew right through the AA fire without a scratch. Lucky for the carriers, they were not "crash divers." Damn, I wonder how long we will continue to cruise around like this?

12 January 1945
At sea

Finally got the word that the beachhead is well secured, and everything is going along nicely without any air attacks.

We are still out here patrolling, and we have gone to GQ several times because of our own planes not turning on their recognition equipment. Everything is fine except for this rough sea. We are bouncing around back and forth. Makes it nice for sleeping.
On the mid-watch: We are still rolling along in an impatient, turbulent sea. We fueled at sea from a tanker which had a baby carrier fueling on the other side of it.

We hop to GQ every morning and at least once in the evening. Our planes land at sunset, so there is no air protection after that.

13 January 1945
At sea

Nothing to report except a carrier lost two planes. One of the pilots was recovered, and I hope the other guy was recovered also. We are still rolling along in a heavy sea at a slow speed. We are waiting for the Japs to come out and fight. I don't think they will until we invade China!

I read excerpts of the *Johnston*, DD557, in the battle of 25 and 26 of October. The Intelligence Magazine gave us a colorful account. In it were excerpts from diaries of Jap flyers. It gave us an interesting view of the Japanese character. The Jap considers it a great honor to die for his Emperor—committing suicide or anything else. They have many enlisted men as pilots in the Japanese Navy and Army.

20 January 1945
At sea

0400: Three unidentified ships were reported in the vicinity. A carrier was designated to have their planes ready for a strike. We'll learn more about this later.

1700: No word as to what the carrier planes did to the unidentified ships. We are patrolling up and down in a rough sea. There are ten carriers out now with four cruisers and us destroyers. There was an operational message in code to COMDESDIV 21 (us). I hope it is orders to proceed to port sometime soon.

21 January 1945
In China Sea

Nothing of interest to report, except the Nips are leaving us alone. We are still patrolling up and down the coast of Luzon. There is a big old beautiful moon up right now, and a nice cool, refreshing breeze. If we weren't rolling so much in this rough sea, it would be pleasant out here. If I remember correctly, Richard Halliburton, the author and adventurer, lost his life in this sea off the coast of China. I believe he was a Memphis lad. I hit upon a crazy idea tonight while in my sack. Being as military training is going to be a compulsion after the war, why not start a Seamanship Academy there in Memphis, on the Mississippi River for boys 14 to 17 years old? Teach them seamanship by ex-enlisted men in the Navy? All rates. Combine this with one of the private schools, and I believe it will be profitable. Just another day dream. Ha!

23 January 1945
China Sea

It seems pretty calm at present. Maybe we are steaming directly in the trough of the Sea? There is nothing new to report. The Japs on Luzon are trapped without supplies, and, apparently, the Jap leaders are not going to try to reinforce them. I don't blame them. With Uncle Sam's Navy steaming up and down the coast, I don't think they want to run the risk. We have excellent recon planes reporting enemy ships in every port on the China coast and those moving in the Jap Empire waters. We are winning! It is nice and smooth sailing now.

24 January 1945
China Sea

There was a lull in the monotony today—if in news only. The *Nicholas* went out to investigate an aircraft report that there was a Jap small craft in the water a short distance away. When our plane dove down, the Japs started waving a Jap flag, thinking the plane was Japanese. When the two of them realized it was an American plane, they hid under a canopy on the fantail of the craft. When the *Nicholas* came alongside, the Japs refused to come aboard. The *Nick* asked permission to use force, but the Commander on the *Phoenix* took over the situation—they hoisted the Japs, boat and all, aboard. The poor chaps knew they had no choice.

The dope on tomorrow's dope sheet says that we may expect to bombard for the next invasion or landing. So, we are going to have a problem. This operation was to end on the 31st!

25 January 1945
China Sea

We were supposed to receive mail yesterday when the *Jenkins* and *LaValette* joined us. I think we are to go to Mindoro for fuel tomorrow; maybe we will pick up some mail then. Mr. Murphy tells us that the *Beale* and its squadron are the luckiest ships to ever come out here. They were in Sydney twice and are now back in the States. I should have stayed aboard the *Beale*—if I hadn't been such an ass!

2130: The *Jenkins* came alongside with 34 bags of mail this afternoon. I didn't get those white socks that I asked my mother to send me. The mail from home makes one think of how nice it will be back in the States!

29 January 1945
China Sea

The days are getting dreadfully monotonous. We have been out here on patrol for almost a month now. We are low on provisions and our main course for food is Spam and rice. There is a possibility that we may go in the 2nd of next month for provisions. Then we will be ready for anther month of patrol duty. Heaven forbid! The cruiser *Denver*, and the *Fletcher* and *Radford*, were selected to make the bombardment on the next landing. I believe the landing will be right above Bataan. Then, I suppose we will be elected to patrol that beachhead. Damn this roll!

Did not get the remainder of my Christmas Packages and only one letter from my mother.

2030: On watch 'til midnight. Having the devil of a time with the radio equipment.

30 January 1945
China Sea

Everything is going along serenely with no excitement. The landing went off smoothly, as was probably expected.

There is a note that I forgot to mention: Lieutenant Commander Franklin D. Roosevelt, Jr., was in command of one of a group of destroyers which were assigned to sink a Jap sub spotted by one of our planes today. We wish him luck.

The chow situation is becoming acute—or already is. When we run out of Spam, things are in a terrible state of affairs. If we go into Mindoro, as we are supposed to do on the 2nd of February, they have dry provisions and mail for us. I am ready to go anywhere as the days are monotonous. All of us are thinking about going home and what we are going to do when we get there.

One of the Crew, USS O'Bannon, World War II

[FDR's Ship, *The Albert C. Moore*, a DE.]

31 January 1945
China Sea

Everything was okay until about 2100 tonight. Then we were called to battle stations. The *Jenkins*, *Bell*, and the *O'Bannon* contacted a sub underwater at the same time with our sonar equipment. He was tracked by radar by several of the ships before he disappeared. (Radar can only pick up anything above the surface.) The three of us made what is believed to be a successful depth charge run. Later, the *Bell*, DD587, made another run, and there were two underwater explosions, and bubbles came to the surface. The Commander of the task force said, "Better get the Captain's shirt so you can get credit for the damned thing." We secured from GQ at about 0230, but "Condition Able" was kept in effect. I have the 0400-to-0800 watch, and I am plenty tired. Have been working out for the past couple of days. I feel I must get in condition.

1 February 1945
Mindoro, P.I.

I hit the sack right after chow this morning and slept 'til 1500.

We came into port about 0600, fueled and anchored. No provisioning this harbor at this time. Man, O Man! We are all tired of corned beef any way it is fixed to eat. We learned today that the *Jenkins*, DD447, one of our Division, received a 75mm hit on its #4 turret, killing three guys immediately, and three more died later.

During the bombardment at Lingayen, the *New Mexico* was hit by a "dive smasher," killing the Captain and Admiral. The cruiser *Louisville* and the Australian cruiser, *Australian*, were also hit, injuring Commodore Collins, who formerly was in command of our Task Force.

2 February 1945
Mindoro, P.I.

Got a good night's sleep until 0700, then on watch. The *Bell*, *Moore*, *Jenkins*, and *O'Bannon* were commended by Commander Seventh Fleet, and given a "well done" for the other night's sinking of the Jap submarine. I guess our depth-charge run was a pretty good one.

This is certainly a swell port, and about the most beautiful Island in the whole group. The harbor is just like glass, with a big old gorgeous moon. It reminds me of some of the old love stories one reads about. Ah, Yes! What a life!

On mid-watch: We were all set for a nice day in port with a movie on the foc's'le. The CDD 21 assigns the *O'Bannon*, *Radford*, and *Jenkins* for a 24-hour patrol outside the harbor. Oh, well, it isn't too bad.

4 February 1945
Patrolling off Mindoro

0400: We thought we would go in, but we have been assigned another day, which means we will probably rotate with the other three ships in our squadron and have two days in port after today. We really look forward to the movies.

Things are looking up these days. The Russians are only 50 or 60 miles from Berlin, and the Nips are being pushed back steadily.

1800: We came into port at about 1430, and we will have a movie on the foc's'le tonight, but, of course, I have the watch at that time. No mail today. Don't know what happened to the delivery service. One hardly feels like writing.

One of the Crew, USS O'Bannon, World War II

5 Feb 1945
Mindoro, P.I.

Late: Yep, it looks like we will patrol two days in and two day out. As yet, we have no chow on board, and I have had enough of corned beef.

We saw a movie tonight that was really a "stinker": Nelson Eddy and Jeanette MacDonald in, "I married an Angel." Gad, how it reeked!

7 Feb 1945
Patrolling off Mindoro

Except for the movies, I had rather be out here. It is cooler. I know I overuse the word "beautiful," but it really is, and a big old moon sets it off.

Still no chow. After tomorrow, we go on a steady diet of beans and green peas three times a day. We were asked by the "boss" how much provisions we had, and our Captain said, "one day."

I have been busy in the radio shack straightening out our files A convoy came in, including the ship with provisions that we have been waiting for, the *Pollux*, a refrigerator ship. Oh. Boy! No more corned beef!

13 Feb 1945
Subic Bay P.I.

I had my boil lanced, and this thing is really sore. In talking with my Pharmacist's Mate buddy, Harper, he said the doctor had something to do with the recent transfers, including our radio-gang member, Miller. He said these guys just could not conquer their fear. Miller was one. Harper said these guys couldn't sleep, nor eat properly. I told him that all hands except radiomen and radar men got more sleep than we did. Anyway, it was for the best.

The Philippine Islands

We had movies on the foc's'le last night with the boom of artillery firing in the background. This is a crazy war. In Pearl Harbor, there is a strict blackout, and they won't even let a boat out after dark, but here with people killing each other a few miles away, we have movies.

I am looking for the OP PLAN for this operation. All of us are supposed to have read it, but I missed out. I want to get all the dope. The Jap shore batteries are all marked off on a map, and our only surface trouble might be PT boats, and Q boats, which carry only one torpedo and a couple of AA guns. The Japs may be waiting for us where it is possible to do the most damage with their guns.

2015: On watch. We went and bombarded Corregidor and Bataan today, and did not receive any return fire. Army A-25 bombers were bombing both places which seem to make our shell fire seem puny by comparison. At one time, Corregidor was completely consumed with smoke and dust. We banged away for about three hours. If there are any Japs over there, and the plan stated that they are, they are really taking a drubbing.

There are two Jap battleships, a few cruisers and destroyers about 300 hundred miles away looking for a chance to come and bombard our positions now. Our Task Group is added to all Urgent messages concerning them. Our planes were sent in for an air strike that did quite a bit of damage, and from the latest reports, we are sending in another air strike at dawn.

Maybe I had better explain today's operation a little better. First, the minesweepers went and did their job out to Corregidor and along the coast of Bataan. The Task Group followed, split in two forces. One bombarded Corregidor, and the other bombarded Bataan. We were in the latter group. It was a great sight to see Corregidor sticking out of the bay like a sore thumb, and our high-altitude bombers smack it with everything they had. Our boys may have taken the same kind of beating a few years ago by the Japs. Tomorrow, we do the same thing. This next time, I hope it will be more interesting. Here in Subic Bay, the guns don't rumble as often as they did. I feel that our guns will continue to keep the Japs terrified—my guess.

Yes—Sherman was right: "War is Hell." How can supposedly-intelligent human beings be so stupid?

14 Feb 1945
Off Bataan

1630: We are bombarding again. Today has really been a busy day, with plenty of Jap return fire. The *Fletcher* took a 3-inch shell in the Chief's quarters, and it disabled Number One 5-inch gun. A minesweeper was sunk by a Jap shore battery. All bombardments looked to be most effective, but the Japs put up a good scrap. We had knocked off at about 1300 hours, but when the *Fletcher* got hit, we came back to bombard both Bataan and Corregidor, from a close distance. The minesweeper that got sunk was right ahead of the *Fletcher*, not too far from us at the time. B-25s and A-20s joined in and are still bombing both Bataan and Corregidor. The Japs are really taking a beating.

At one time the shells from our cruisers were flying over Corregidor, and they landed very near the *Hopewell*, who now has COMDESDIV 21 aboard.

Upon our return to port (if we do), we have been assigned to patrol duty outside of Subic Bay, which means we will have no movies tonight. We are getting the lousy end with these patrol duty assignments.

The Jap battleships and the other Jap ships that were sighted about 300 miles away were hit on two attacks by our planes. They have retired to Formosa. That isn't safe waters for them by any means. Don't know the results yet.

1815: The *LaValette* struck a mine while bombarding close in to the beach, and the crew is abandoning ship. I saw one explosion.

and we are going to assist. WAIT A MINUTE—it is the *Radford* that struck the mine; both were in the same position. Details later.

15 Feb 1945
At sea

Here are the details. The *LaVallette* went into a little cove on Bataan to get a closer bead on a Jap shore battery and hit the mine. The *Radford* immediately went to her assistance, and hit a mine also. The *Radford*'s TBS equipment is dead, so don't know her disposition, however, the *Radford* backed out of the cove under her own power. Three minesweepers towed the *LaVallette* out to where we were. She is really fouled up and low at the bow. The crew jettisoned everything they could to make her lighter in the water. The *Hopewell* took a 3-inch shell through her #1 stack. Boy, this used to be a lucky division, but that makes four hit in one day. The *Taylor*, *Nicholas*, and *O'Bannon* remain unscathed.

Off Corregidor

1020: Mr. Murphy told us how the *Hopewell* made out. She received four 4-inch hits, killing one officer and seven enlisted men. It was much more serious than I thought.

There we go! We are firing now.

1045: We are receiving plenty of return fire this morning. Bowman ran down from the bridge and said, "When they start firing at the *O'Bannon*, it's time to get off the bridge in a hurry!" Two Jap salvos went right over us. We must be in pretty close. We are bottled up in the radio shack and can't see what's going on. The *Phoenix*, which has the Commander of the Task Group aboard, is firing at Jap gun positions set in heavy masonry. There are quite a few well-placed Jap shore batteries around here. The first wave of troops go in in an hour and twenty minutes.

1140: We have two waves of troops on Bataan with no opposition, next to the beach. I guess the Japs took to the hills.

A-20s, P-38s and B-24s are pasting Corregidor with everything, along with the cruisers and destroyers. It hardly seems possible that anything is left living on that place. However, every time we come in, they give us some return fire. The A-20s are skip bombing and strafing at random now, and we are in close and can hear the machine guns chattering as the planes fly over.

Everyone seems to be pleased with LT(j.g.) Huck, the fire control officer. He puts our shells right where they do the most good. The whole fire control crew should be commended; Huck doesn't do it all by himself. Our fire control group silenced several Jap shore batteries this morning. God knows, they have had enough practice. The paratroops will land on Corregidor tomorrow. A LSM ran into a mine and sank during today's operations. We knocked off at noon, while the cruisers keep banging away at Corregidor. Our troops are well situated on Bataan.

16 Feb 1945
Entering Subic Bay

The paratroopers landed on Corregidor today—about 3,000 of them—in an all-day operation. Some of them were killed because their chutes would not open. We bombarded before they landed, and covered the minesweeps, which was fun, because we had to stay at GQ all day. We went into the bay close enough to see Manila off in the distance. The *Nicholas* was hit by eight 40mm shells today, wounding one man. Last night, the minesweeps were fired on at Montevedas right where we landed the troops. The Japs had guns on boats and hit several of the minesweepers.

A funny thing happened today. The *Claxton* found herself in the middle of a mine field with about 20 mines around her, and she couldn't get out. The crew couldn't hit the things with rifle fire to explode them. How she got out, I will never know.

Several of the paratroopers landed in the sea and were picked up by our PT Boats. There still is no news in regard to the *LaValette* and *Radford* casualties. We are going in now for fuel and ammunition, which we badly need. We may run out of chow and other necessities, but never out of fuel and ammunition!

17 Feb 1945
Subic Bay

We will take on ammunition this morning, which is an all-hands job. I don't know how we are managing to stay in port. It certainly isn't because we have a big drag with the boss. Would just as soon be at sea.

Some sadistic ass threw the movie screen over the side, and the Exec said we won't have movies until it reappears. Gad, how silly!

We will get underway with the cruiser *Cleveland*, and the *Nicholas* and the *Taylor* early in the AM. Must be something going on as the commanders of all the ships are to have a meeting aboard the *Cleveland* before we go.

The talk about going to the States has died down. It stands to reason that the Destroyer Division 21 are warships, and we are at war, with experienced crews, which is needed to win this war. It is a Navy war to a huge extent. So, I can understand why the "Brass" would not want to send us home in the middle of the action.

The *Cleveland* plane (a two-seater, single-prop unit called a "Kingfisher") spotted for us and the *Taylor* to bombard the territory, with 200 Japs there. In Zapang village, 200 Japs; San Jose village, 150 Japs; Tangaran village, 1000 Japs and an Ammunition Dump. They weren't supposed to have any native civilians there, but during the bombardment, women and children ran out of the houses waving American flags, as was reported by the spotting plane. Of course, that could be a Jap ruse but I don't think so. The Patriots did not agree with me and did not stop the bombardment. We expended fifty rounds per gun, which was allotted.

Our movie screen has not shown up, and no one will squeal on the so-and-so that did it. He should be Shot at Sunrise!

19 Feb 1945
Subic Bay

This has been a comfortable day. I worked on my files this morning and took a sunbath on the fantail.

We have been assigned to DESDIV 42, along with the *Fletcher* and *Jenkins* for the next operation. Whatever that is.

The *Fletcher* had funeral services for the guy that got killed the other day when she was hit. The *Hopewell* is on its way for repairs, and the *Radford* and *LaValette* will go also when they are able to get underway.

20 Feb 1945
Subic Bay

Butler and I went over to Grande Island (the name of the island dividing the entrance to the bay) for some relaxation and our three beers.

There is ammunition all over the place lying out in the open, magazines that didn't explode during a terrific bombardment. There are projectiles and powder all over. A couple of lads off one of the cruisers were killed when they triggered a Jap "booby trap" in the ruins. Three more were wounded, one having lost a hand. I didn't see the guys, but heard the explosion. It spoiled the afternoon. Some of the dopey asses were burning the bags of powder to see them go up in flames. All of us were warned to stay away from the ammunition. But that is like telling a kid, "I double dare you!"

21 Feb 1945
Subic Bay

Had burial services for the two boys who were killed yesterday. They were part of the crew on the *Montpelier*.

Received an Urgent message that the *Renshaw* was torpedoed. It was the destroyer that we tied up alongside in Tulagi.

Movies have been resumed on the Foc's'le starting tonight. Never did find out who threw the screen over the side. Got 21 bags of mail a few minutes ago.

22 Feb 1945
Subic Bay

Received a letter, written on the 18th of January, that my brother, Norman is missing in action. It is quite a blow and leaves me all mixed up. Somehow, I cannot believe that he is dead—not my brother Norman—who is a credit to the human race! But, I suppose other people feel the same way about their loved ones. Then too, when Norman went into the Army, I felt something like this might happen. He volunteered—with a wife and two kids. Only the good men die young—-not guys like me who live to raise hell the rest of our days. I won't give up hope. God knows I hope he is okay.

No news from home. I want to hear about Norman. We are going to sea tomorrow. I would like to get some mail before we leave. I had a run-in with Zarnecki today. He is a wise-ass kid feeling his oats. He hands out a lot of guff, and is not willing to take orders. He is always knocking the officers, and refers to the Exec as a "Jew Bastard." I didn't waste my time arguing with him. I will let Mr. Murphy handle the matter.

24 Feb 1945
At sea

We left Subic at about 1730, on our way to Mindoro to pick up assault troops to invade Palawan. No opposition is expected. We have the *Fletcher*, *Jenkins*, and *Abbot* destroyers, and the cruisers *Denver*, *Montpelier*, and *Cleveland* in the group. Palawan is an oblong island southwest of Mindoro and on the extreme western side of the Philippines. They intend to establish an air base there, in addition to Mindoro.

Still no news about Norman. We received mail aboard too. I feel confident that he is a prisoner. Out of his regiment, there were 426 killed, over 1,000 wounded, and 7,001 missing, who could be prisoners of war. Good Lord! I hope he is among these.

26 Feb 1945
Mindoro, P.I.

We arrived here yesterday morning and are waiting for the assault troops to get loaded on the landing crafts. This a pretty harbor with the moon at night, and the sea is always calm, and makes the place pleasant for anchorage.

Still no news about that brother of mine. I have almost refused to worry, as I am quite confident that he is a prisoner of war. Maybe it is God's means of keeping him safe.

Very much later. We get the breaks of the squadron, believe me! We were assigned to harbor patrol, which we are doing in a military manner at present. We also have "morning alert" and later GQ to test all batteries. What a lousy, rotten pain in the cookie! Always when I have the mid-watch!

28 Feb 1945
En route Palawan

0630: We are to be the standby ships and screen for the cruisers as they bombard, which starts at 0715, and "H" hour troops land at 0845 at Puerto Princesa. No opposition in great strength is expected. We leave here about noon, if everything proceeds according to plan, and arrive at Subic Bay sometime tomorrow.

1 March 1945
En route Mindoro

We were steaming along pleasantly when John Artisani picked up a sub contact. We made a few runs and dropped depth charges. The Task Force Commander ordered us to pick up freight at Mindoro after we were relieved by DE's, which was about 0200. The DE's picked up the contact also, For awhile, we thought we had sunk the sub, as an oil slick came to the surface. Of course, that is an old trick. The DE's will probably get it.

3 March 1945
Subic Bay

Still no news about Norman. I am getting more concerned every day, and suppose I am harder to get along with. Just a note here and there from the family.

The boys on the bridge are confident that we will be going back to the States soon. I bet five bucks that we won't till the war is over. Three destroyers from DESDIV 23 have been assigned to our division to fill in for the *Radford*, *Hopewell*, and *LaValette*. That looks bad. It means the Brass has something for us to do.

4 March 1945
Subic Bay

We are off again tonight for Mindoro to pick up troops for another landing. Ziegler, a quartermaster, informed me the target is Mindanao, and also our last operation! Can it be possible? It is doubtful that we would go back to the States. Instead, we may join Admiral Spruance's Fifth Fleet. Whichever we do, we shouldn't be out here much longer.

Mid-watch: After a very warm day in port, we got underway with our squadron, with the new ships temporarily assigned, and the *Phoenix* and *Boise* headed for Mindoro. We will probably be there for a couple of days, then off to invade Mindanao, the richest of all the Philippine Islands.

One of the Crew, USS O'Bannon, World War II

6 March 1945
Mindoro

We lay at anchor all day yesterday, and it looks like we will remain here all day today. I managed to answer all my back mail. My romance has ended, because I cannot be there to take care of the romance. It looks like the old Lee boy will remain single. Still no news about my brother Norman. God, please don't keep us waiting much longer.

We are off to Zamboanga, where the monkeys have no tails, tomorrow morning. The Japs have two 6-inch guns that we know we must contend with. In addition, there are several 3-inch batteries. We don't know exactly where they are. All-in-all, it should be an easy operation—so Murphy says.

8 March 1945
At sea

0300: We are nearing our objective, the Zamboanga area on the island of Mindanao. They tell us that we can expect mines, 6- and 8-inch shore batteries, suicide planes, and submarines. We will bombard previous to the landing on the 10th. This doesn't look like it is going to be an easy "pushover" at all!

1700: We came in behind the minesweepers, which did not dig up a single mine. Liberators bombed the hell out of targets that were selected. One of the cruisers and two of our destroyers started to bombard in one area, and the natives came down to the beach waving American flags. The bombardment stopped. We cruised up and down the beach trying to draw enemy fire. It was in vain. Two Moro natives came out in an outrigger canoe. We picked one of them up. He said there weren't any Japs over there. We shall see. So far we have not fired a shot.

9 March 1945
Zamboanga Bay

We have been cruising up an down the beach all morning shooting at nothing that I could see worth shooting at. We did knock up a lot of dirt. The B-24s are really bombing hell out of the place. Right now we are firing at a 3-inch shore battery that was hidden behind a house. One of the cruisers put several salvos into it. The Jap battery was firing at a British survey ship, which was measuring the depth of the bay, and fired at one of the minesweepers. Why the survey ship was there, I have no idea. I am not told everything. We are working with the *Phoenix* and the *Jenkins;* the other group is the *Boise, Abbot,* and *Fletcher.*

1100: The Japs just shot down one of the B-24s. It burst into flames. No parachutes were seen. At least we know that there are Japs over there, and we are doing some damage. Correction here—one of the B-24s ran into a load of bombs dropped by a buddy. The Japs had nothing to do with it. I did not see any AA bursts. During the afternoon, all ships including the minesweepers, except the cruisers, cruised along the coast blasting away. We received some Jap return fire that was quickly silenced. The city of Zamboanga is now a mass of flaming wreckage. Fires continue to burn as we go out to sea. The assault troops are to land in the morning. We will probably be around for the next couple of days.

10 March 1945
Zamboanga Bay

Everything has gone off according to plan. We bombarded up until time for the troops to land. After they landed, A-20 planes made low-level bombing and strafing runs over the Jap positions. We were close to the beach and had a good view of all the action.
1300: We are standing by now to give fire support if needed. The *Taylor* got into a spat with a shore battery. It was well hidden, but not accurate. It managed to get a few close shots at an LST and the *Taylor.* A B-25 bomber flew right over us and dropped delayed action bombs over the whole area. After that, silence prevailed. A-20s and B-25s strafed and bombed all afternoon. The explosions

caused devastating damage. I looked over the city with a glass, and I could not see a living soul but did see a few air-raid shelters. A few natives came out in canoes from a shanty village.

11 March 1945
Zamboanga Bay

Noon: We have had a busy morning after all. After we secured from "Morning Alert," we were called to GQ at 1000 as four shore batteries were laying their shots close to the *Taylor*—again! Later there were six shore batteries. We steamed in, and our fire control crew headed up by LT(j.g.) Huck knocked out four of them! Great shooting for this young officer.

The Japs managed to hit one of our fuel supplies. It is still burning. We received a "Well Done" from Admiral Royal, who is in charge of the operation. It looked like we got four of the guns, but when the plane spotter came down, he said we destroyed three, and silenced the other three. Not bad! There was quite a bit of mortar fire on the landing. We crept too close to the beach in certain areas.

12 March 1945
En route Mindoro

Our mission is finished—with several congratulatory messages known as "verbal grab ass." All ships in the operation received a "well done" from Admiral Royal. We are scheduled for one more operation in the Philippines, maybe two, and we should be in port for about a week.

We go in for mail. I do hope I have some concerning brother Norman.

13 March 1945
At sea

We arrived at Mindoro about noon. Fueled and waited for the other ships to take on ammunition (we loaded up on ammunition from a LST at Zamboanga). Now we are underway at 1900 for Subic Bay.

Tomorrow we will fire for PRACTICE! Yep, the sleeves will be drawn by the observation planes on the cruisers. Incidentally, the pilots on the cruiser planes said the guns we knocked out at Zamboanga were 155mm, which is almost a 6-inch gun. Fine shooting! I forgot to mention, the Japs tried to mine Zamboanga harbor at night. A sailing craft was picked up with three mines aboard.

Murphy said we would be in port for about a week unless we get patrol duty, which is most likely.

17 March 1945
Subic Bay

These last few days have been swell. We are tied up alongside the destroyer tender *Dobbin*, which assumed all the radio shack communication duties.

21 March 1945
Subic Bay

We pulled away from the tender this morning and anchored. Our next operation is coming up day after tomorrow. I copied the orders this evening. While alongside the *Dobbin*, we accomplished some much-needed things. I calibrated the transmitters and installed a receiver in Radio Central. Had a good field day. Did some cleaning and painting. Fixed a good practice system for operating, etc. We could easily do another year out here as far as the radio communications department is concerned.

John Cutler and I have been doing a little material work together— good work too! Since the orders were in code, I don't know where the next operation will be, but suppose it will be at Mindanao, Dumanquiles Bay. A guess. I understand it will not be a serious operation. Or, it could be the China Coast!! ????

One of the Crew, USS O'Bannon, World War II

22 March 1945
Subic Bay

Our day of sailing has been set up or back 24 hours which means we will have another day of peace. The nights have been ideal, with a beautiful moon shining: everything an artist or nature lover would enjoy.

I pray daily for my brother Norman. Somehow, I know that he is alive in some German prison camp. God grant it!

24 March 1945
At sea

We are on our way to land on Cebu. We are with the *Nicholas* and the cruiser *Phoenix*. There are supposed to be some 3-inch and 76mm, and also some AA guns, to contend with. We will be the fire support force prior to the invasion hour. Several of our crew have asked me if there is any news about going home. I do not expect we will anytime soon. I pray that my mother has news about Norman. Dear God, please don't keep us in suspense much longer!

26 March 1945
At sea

The landing begins this morning. The *O'Bannon* will start bombarding at 0715. We have to be on the lookout for suicide boats and shore batteries. These suicide boats are pretty fast. They will do about 35 knots, and they carry a very large depth charge right in the boat with a one-man crew. The guy will explode the depth charge as it hits the ship.

We received a new batch of "V" records with 20 of the latest tunes by the best bands in the land. Harry James, Glenn Miller, Frank Sinatra, Bing Crosby, Duke Ellington and Spike Jones—many more. We have Andre Kostelanetz on the speaker system. Good music.

0900: Everything is going according to plan. The barrage was really terrific. This old baby shook and trembled in every seam. Two LCIs cruised along just off the beach, tossing rockets, which have a terrific concussion. We have landed the troops this side of the city, which is a handsome one. It looks like something an artist would paint. All seems quiet except for the occasional crack of the cruisers' gun fire, which are lying well off shore. I think this was the heaviest barrage of all our landings. We secured from GQ, to be called back again as three Jap planes had taken off from the airstrip. Probably they were taking the Jap high command to safer ground.

27 March 1945
At sea

That show didn't last long. We joined our task force and started on our way back last night. Before we left, we could see fires in the city. Evidently the Japs put their demolition squads to work. The last report was that our force had not entered the city yet. The landing went well. I hate to see a beautiful city such as Cebu ruined.

I am getting sore at this Exec. He has never been popular with the crew. Personality has nothing to do with it. As far as I am concerned, he has too many unnecessary regulations. Such as being in complete uniform before leaving or entering a port, including hats! It is the Navy way, which I have always hated!

30 March 1945
Subic Bay

Yesterday, two destroyers went with some men from each ship in the task force to Manila on a sight-seeing tour. We sent 17 men from the *O'Bannon*. We were supposed to have gone up today with more men, but the Task Force Commander called it off until Monday. Maybe they have something better in store for us? I really want to go!

Great News! My brother Norman is safe!

He is a prisoner of war in Germany. Much better than missing in action. I hope he is physically okay and not wounded. I just had a hunch he would be all right and he would be in some prison camp. Bob Butler, my best friend aboard this ship, has a brother who is in a Nazi prison camp also.

31 March 1945
Subic Bay

They called off the trips to Manila until Monday. Today is Saturday.

I talked to Murphy and Bowman about having a letter written to Washington to rate me in excess. They said they would see; however, I doubt very seriously if anything will be done about it. I'm getting pretty disgusted—no, it's past that; I'll say "fed up." I think I'll try to be transferred to the beach, get a swap or something. It shouldn't be hard as we are to go back soon. Anybody would jump at the chance. A little duty around here might do me good.

The "limeys" have joined us now, a landing on Okinawa is expected soon. Maybe it's today. Just hope this war doesn't last much longer.

2 April 1945
Subic Bay

We are scheduled to go to Manila Wednesday and Thursday, or be there during that time.

This is pretty nice lying at anchor in a harbor as cool and comfortable as this.

Murphy has us copying headings of messages in search of intelligence summaries. It isn't hard to do, just bothersome. According to the Squadron Commander, we have "the best communication department in the squadron." We are well experienced. The new men on the other ships are being trained to relieve the "old timers."

3 April 1945
Subic Bay

We leave tomorrow morning for Manila for sightseeing tours. I think I'll go over and look the place over.

There seems to be dissension in the Radio gang again. Everyone is sore at Murphy because of this extra watch on the Honolulu schedule expressly for news. We seem to think he is "banging ears" at our expense. One man cannot stay off watch during the movies—except Honaker. Murphy took care of that—he secured the sked long enough for his boy to go. I've seen many a raw deal in my time, but never have I seen favoritism like this.

If I get as disgusted as I was before, I'm afraid something is going to pop somewhere if I have to blow the lid off the whole rotten set-up.

4 April 1945
Manila, P.I.

Well, here we are! There are about 30 or 40 sunken ships still visible. The masts and some superstructures are above the water. A cruiser, two destroyers, and a bunch of merchant ships or cargo vessels. I am on the liberty list tomorrow and have the watch this afternoon. I am really anxious to hear more about this place and see this beautiful and modern city.

5 April 1945
Subic Bay

We just came in from Manila, a three-hour trip. I saw some things today that I will remember the rest of my life. We went ashore as though we were having an inspection. Clean shaven, white uniforms, shined shoes, etc. The "Brass" want the Filipinos to know that the U. S. Navy is back!

One of the Crew, USS O'Bannon, World War II

Manila is just one big junk pile! Big buildings gutted by bombs; houses, churches, theatres—all a big pile of rubble. Automobiles wrecked and shot full of holes. Ships sunk alongside the docks—lots of ships. There was one big war in Manila proper. Ruins that can never be repaired, in my estimation.

I talked with two very pretty Filipino girls who said they hid out in the mountains, and they have a sister in the internment camp here who is married to an American and will go to the States soon.

I must admire these people—they are American to the core. In addition, they manage to keep clean and neat. Well-starched clothing; and the men look like they had just left a barber shop. Of course there were some grubby-looking natives also. There are many houses of ill repute, and liquor is available. Some of our guys tried each vice. I went over with Mr. Murphy—there were 19 of us altogether. We went sightseeing! Inflation had taken over. We paid 50 cents for a bottle of pop, put up in coke bottles, which was a cross between root beer and what tasted like salt water.

Only God knows why people could destroy this once-beautiful city! I picked up some souvenirs, Dutch, Chinese, and Philippine money, and there was Japanese invasion currency scattered all over the streets. I picked up some of that too.

8 April 1945
Subic Bay

Our carrier planes hit a Japanese task force consisting of one battleship, three cruisers, and nine destroyers. The last report was that a cruiser and one destroyer got away. The last OFFICIAL dope was: Our planes sank four destroyers and a cruiser. The battleship and four destroyers were burning fiercely.

Tonight, while on the mid-watch, our force was called out to intercept three Jap ships very close in our area. Five of our cruisers, and nine destroyers, went out after them. We could not go because we were taking aboard new torpedoes, and they were not ready to fire yet. We will know the results soon.

10 April 1945

For the past two days we have been playing "cops and robbers" with all hands at GQ. All of us had rather be in action than continue to train and train! It is indeed a pain in the fanny. We had enough of the training at Treasury. The *Nicholas* and the *O'Bannon* are to escort the *Phoenix* into the beach at El Fraile. This is where the concrete battleship is mounted on an island at the entrance to Manila Bay. We don't know the reason yet, but we heard that a few Japs were holed up there. So, we will shoot them out!

11 April
Subic Bay

We still have the Australian soldiers aboard. These guys have been through hell fighting the Germans and Italians in Italy. Max Cook and Darby Wells hang around the radio shack and drink coffee. I think we switched them from drinking tea.

We are always in training. We fired at a sleeve for practice this morning, then proceeded to El Fraile and the concrete battleship. We still don't know why the *Phoenix* went there. We are always in a guessing game. On the beach, a P-51 fighter plane took a nosedive. We sent a whaleboat with our doctor over there, but there wasn't much left. Don't know how long we are going to hang around this place. I know we won't be going home any time soon. I think the "brass" thinks that we are too good at what we do, and we are needed to win this war. We sure as hell have had enough practice doing what we do. Speaking of practice, there is wind of another training cruise in the offing. Gad! What a horrible fate! I would much rather be in the thick of a war zone than go through one of those again!

15 April 1945
En route to Subic Bay

The *Phoenix*, *Nicholas*, and *O'Bannon* bombarded Curabao this morning for a couple of hours to prepare for a landing there. We banged away at several emplacements with no return fire that I know of, as we are bottled up in the radio shack during GQ. I suppose we will be here to back up the landing tomorrow. After that, we will do some more firing for practice. What a pain!

On the old mid-watch. We get underway tomorrow at 0500 to again bombard Curabao for the landing at 0900 and will return to port at 1400, provided that we don't run into any trouble. Three hundred and fifty Japs are expected to be on that barren place with tall bluffs.

Too bad our President had to die in the middle of this war. He had my full support as the most able man for the job. I sincerely pray that Harry Truman can fill his shoes!

[President Franklin Delano Roosevelt died on 12 April 1945. Vice president Harry S. Truman became president of the United States.]

16 April 1945
Subic Bay

We bombarded for the landing this morning. We had a soldier on board with a walkie-talkie radio for communicating with the Army on the beach, and to help direct gun fire. Swell fellow too. After the soldiers landed, they told us that no Japs were found, but forgot the "colors" (flag), and asked if they could come out tomorrow in a landing craft to borrow a set of colors from us. Now the flag from the *O'Bannon* flies over Curabao! We came in about 1700 this evening. This is really the life.

I read an intelligence dispatch yesterday: 14 dive smashers dived on one ship near Okinawa. Four of them hit; the others missed. There were 58 suicide bombers in all that attacked our force, and several of the ships were damaged. (My old ship, *William D. Porter*, DD579, was sunk at Okinawa.)

The Philippine Islands

17 April 1945
Subic Bay

We went this morning for AA practice; came back in at about 1300.

There is an air of dissension among the radio shack personnel right now. Butler, Cutler and Boyte fouled up a summary this morning due to a bad signal. Bowman called us all in to give us hell. He seemed disappointed when he learned that I had nothing to do with the problem, and looked for something else to blame me. I told him off, and told him that if he expected good results that he should start setting a good example, and the next time he tried to accuse me of anything that he had better back it up. He was quiet after my little speech.

Here is a comment which impressed me at the time:

> The inspirations of a fighting man.
> They who scorned the thought of my strength
> Except their own to lean on,
> Learned at length,
> How fear can sabotage the bravest heart,
> And human weakness answering the prod,
> Of terror calls, "Help us, Oh God!"
>
> When silence lets the silent voice be heard,
> Bringing its message like a spoken word,
> Believe, believe in Me,
> Cast out your fear.
> I am not up there beyond the sky,
> But here, here in your heart.
> I am the strength you seek,
> Believe!
> And they believed.
>
> Anonymous

One of the Crew, USS O'Bannon, World War II

19 April 1945
Subic Bay, P.I.

Butler and I went over to Grande Island, played softball, swam, and nearly smothered in dust. When we came back, I went on watch. I am plenty tired. It seems like I am sore in every muscle.

I suppose my brother Frank and his wife, Alice, are welcoming a new babe into the world. Would like to be there. Frank is a lucky sailor. He is stationed in Oakland, CA, with the Naval Air Transportation Service (NATS). The news today stated that the Navy lost more men than the Army and Marines combined in the Okinawa operation. The dive smashers (we still did not know to call them Kamikazes) must have had a picnic. Poor stupid people. They must be animals to do such a thing as to do that in such desperation.

Woe is me! I feel like I am 90 years old!

22 April 1945
Subic Bay

I missed the last watch because of a boil—just when I thought I was through with them. The doctor seems perplexed.

We took six Australian soldiers and an officer who are to be spotters in the next operation. (I do not remember what happened to the other six Aussies). In talking to them, they don't know where we are going, and neither do we. A USO show is going to be on Grande Island with Irving Berlin's "This is the Army." I won't go.

23 April 1945
Subic Bay

We will be leaving tomorrow morning to our next operation. Scuttlebutt is flying around that it will be Borneo. We will probably be involved for the whole operation in freeing the Dutch East Indies. We cannot join the Fifth Fleet without a Radar Jammer and a new type director, so I am told. I suppose Sumatra will follow with the next operation. We have the Aussies pretty comfortable and making them at home. They are learning some American slang expressions.

We received new men from the States, seven of them are torpedomen. It is depressing to know that we won't be going home for awhile, but it is no real surprise. We will be out here until the end of the war. We are good at what we do.

2230: Got the straight dope form Mr. Murphy: The operation will be at Tarakan, Borneo.

26 April 1945
At sea

Ah, this been a pleasant trip so far. The sea is smooth as glass, and we are plodding steadily through it.

Have become acquainted with the Australians. They seem to like hanging around the Radio Shack. They like the coffee too, instead of tea. They have been almost all over the world. El Alemain, etc. They envy the Americans and the equipment that we are able to produce; the best of everything, etc. It seems to make them realize that they have unlimited possibilities and opportunities in their own country after the war.

27 April 1945
At sea

Yesterday evening we passed the island of Towi Towi—I think that is the way it is spelled. The *Taylor* picked up six Japs in a barge (landing craft). There were two barges, but the other one blew themselves up. What foolish people!

I have been spending quite a bit of time with Max Cook (I was wrong about the name of the other Aussie in previous segments about Aussie soldiers aboard—I was going by memory). Max is a fine fellow. He has been in the Aussie Army since 1939. Was at Tobruk, El Alemain, Crete, Greece, and in the New Guinea operations. He can and does talk about everything. (I corresponded with him after the war. He became a "solicitor"—a salesman—in Australia after the war.) He doesn't express it, but it seems that he is a great admirer of Americans. The ship's crew do try to keep these guys entertained. We should reach our objective tomorrow..

P.S. We had six Aussie soldiers on the New Guinea operations for the same reason, and going from memory, I had placed Max Cook in one of those. Both groups of Aussies like to hang out at the radio shack and drink coffee.

28 April 1945
Off coast of Tarakan, Borneo

We have been patrolling up and down the coast all day. Our bombardment was delayed because the minesweepers had not finished sweeping all the areas. The cruisers lobbed a few rounds inside the beach. Oil fires are still raging from yesterday's bombing by our planes. The weather has been great, but terribly hot. The sea is like glass, with a gorgeous moon at night. We are wondering if we will have to stick with the liberation of the entire Dutch East Indies? It will take several more months. It looks like the "Aussies" will do it with our Naval support. Oh, well, we may as well do as much as we can, while we can. The war looks good on the other side. Our boys have joined the Russians.

29 April 1945
Off Borneo Coast

We are still patrolling, and expect to shell the beach today, but rain has interfered, and our bosses are afraid it will spoil the spotting.

1 May 1945
Tarakan Bay—anchored

After we bombarded yesterday, the Australian troops landed without any great opposition at 0830. The *Jenkins*, DD447, a member of our squadron, struck a mine yesterday but managed to move underway under its own power for a while anyway. She is tied up alongside the *Phoenix*. That whittles off another of our

The Philippine Islands

Destroyer Division. The *LaValette* received orders to return to the States. Wish we could join her. We are to remain at anchor, and be on call if the "Aussies" need any fire support. Each ship has been designated to cover a certain area.

B-25s went up for a bombing and strafing attack yesterday. Oil fires are still raging from the bombardment and the bombing. Hitler was just announced dead on the radio.

2 May 1945
Tarakan, Borneo

We were called on for fire support this morning, but the *Fletcher* beat us to the draw, and was assigned instead. We took on fuel and ammunition today and relieved the *Taylor* as a fire-support ship. We are still waiting to be called upon in case the "Aussies" run into trouble.

Two of the minesweepers were sunk by Jap shellfire this afternoon. These little Jap devils still have mischief in them.

The *Fletcher* and *Sigourney* will join the *LaValette* on the its way back to the States. The *Sigourney* and *Fletcher* are in good shape, and are not in desperate need of repairs. What about the *O'Bannon*?? The news looks good about the war on the other side, and we are doing well over here. God grant that this war will not last much longer.

3 May 1945
At sea

We are on our way back now to await the next operation, which is the last, we hope. Ha! This going back to the States is really getting to be a joke!

The Australians were making good headway over on Tarakan, and were only 800 yards from the Jap airstrip. Land mines prevented them from using tanks. The destroyer fire knocked out quite a few of the Jap heavy shore batteries. We went alongside the *Jenkins* to take off part of her ammunition. The *Jenkins* is a mess. Completely covered with fuel oil, and so were the crew. It won't be long before the *Jenkins* will be ordered back to the States.

I have struck up quite a friendship with two of our "Aussie" passengers. I find them to be very nice guys. Max "Cookie" Cook, and Ronald "Darby" Wells are their names.

5 May 1945
Subic Bay

We came into port this afternoon after an antiaircraft shoot practice where the *O'Bannon* made the best score. We shot down two sleeves and the *Nicholas* got one. There were five sleeves towed over us. We do have an excellent fire control crew, headed up by LT(j.g.) Huck. It is no wonder that we can't go to the States, our guys shoot too well!

Received mail aboard. I didn't get much, but the news I got was wonderful! Brother Norman is safe and in England, and by now, on his way home. God surely answers prayer!

6 May 1945
Subic Bay, P.I.

Not much to write about these days. We are lying at anchor. The conversations among our sailors is all about going home.

A new Radioman 2/C (second class) came aboard today, which means a transfer is in order, which will be me or Butler, or possibly Honaker. He is older than the rest of us about 28 or 29 years old.

Our "Aussie" friends are still with us, which means we will probably support the Australian troops in another operation.

7 May 1945
Subic Bay

Max Cook, my Aussie friend, said they would be aboard for another three weeks, which means something is scheduled.. My morale needs a boost. Had a good movie about the life of Mark Twain.

9 May 1945
Subic Bay

Yesterday we received word that the war is over—over there! President Truman announced the news in his address to the nation last night. That brings a partial peace to this old world.

The Philippines will be the next aircraft station that will send thousands of bombers to smack Tokyo, and all of Japan, 24 hours a day. What a sin to contemplate death like that, but I feel the Japanese deserve it.

11 May 1945
Subic Bay

The news looks great on the other side. Maybe peace will come to pass over here too? Then what?

I went over to the destroyer tender *Dobbin* to pick up some Confidential and Secret publications with Murphy. It was a short boat ride, but I got sunburned on my face and arms. The new radioman is a nice fellow. Has a few years in college but is incompetent in performing our line of work at this time. He will get the hang of it. At 29 years old, he looks his age.

12 May 1945
Subic Bay

We have a busy week ahead of us. A military inspection occurs in the spring of every year, if feasible. We are to go out Tuesday for drills, including damage control problems. Thursday, we go out for practice torpedo runs, and antiaircraft practice. We continue to train!

After we sharpen up, we are ready for the next operation supporting the Australians, which I think is Balikapan, Borneo.

Can't figure out why I haven't received a letter from home. With Norman there, their time is pretty well occupied.

14 may 1945
Subic Bay

Received the news that my brother Frank and his wife, Alice, are now parents of a son. The Lee family is beginning to grow. The rainy season has begun here. It makes the days cooler, but I miss that big old moon at night.

It is my understanding that we will not be involved in the next operation. "Limey" (British) units have taken our place. This suits me fine, but I had rather be doing something than sitting in port.

We are preparing for the annual military inspection, which means the Commodore inspects the efficiency of each ship. Not much to it in war time, but it was a pain in the fanny during peace time.

15 May 1945
Subic Bay

Commodore Ginder, COMDESDIV 21 (Commander Destroyer Division) made the annual military inspection today. All went well, battle problem and all. We go out tomorrow to fire "fish" (torpedoes) on practice runs. Probably the Task Force Commander will be in charge.

Rumors are that the *Taylor* has orders to go back to the States. If so, that leaves the *O'Bannon* and *Nicholas* in the Division. The rain has really set in, but it let up long enough to have movies on the foc's'le in the evening.

Joe Sweda, my Yeoman buddy that helps with my *Scuttlebutt* news sheet, told me that our former Captain Smith received the Legion of Merit for his service aboard the *O'Bannon*. That was in the news in the States that he was to be given some kind of award for doing such a good job defending the *British Columbia Express* on the way to Leyte.

18 May 1945
Subic Bay P.I.

We are going to sea this morning to screen the tanker *Salamonie* for some kind of practice operation. We went out yesterday to fire a "fish," but the sea was so rough, they were afraid they would lose the danged thing.

There are rumors that we are going to Manila for liberty next week, which is likely since three cruisers and six destroyers went yesterday morning. We will go when they return. Learned yesterday that my brother Norman is home! I wish I could join him there. God has been good to us!

We are waiting for a message to tell us whether we are going home, or to Okinawa. The deadline is tomorrow sometime. Can it possibly be home? I am holding my breath!

20 May 1945
Subic Bay

We received no message sending us home. Murphy received his orders today to go to the War College. Honaker took a swing at me today, and I had to whack him. We are too closely associated; disagreements will happen, but never do they come to blows.

The message we received yesterday states that we shall be detached from the 7th Fleet on the 25th of May, then we will either go join the 5th Fleet around Okinawa or head for the States. All of us are holding our breath! The suspense will probably ruin our liberty in Manila. Mr. Underhill is our new Communications Officer.

We are going to Manila tomorrow for an "unchaperoned" liberty from 0930 to 1800 for two days. I am looking forward to the liberty as I really need some kind of diversion.

25 May 1945
Manila Bay

This brings to a close two fine days of liberty in Manila. Butler and I took in the sights, of night clubs, and walked in alleys which were at one time streets. We found good food in the Chinese area of Manila where there seemed to be no war damage. We were dressed in white uniforms, ready for inspection. Some disheveled soldiers living in pup tents on the banks of the Pasig River waved their olive drab handkerchiefs at us and yelled, "Yoo-hoo girls," which we ignored. Every bridge on the Pasig River had been destroyed. The Filipinos had confiscated American Jeeps and painted them with wild colors and were using them as taxi cabs, which we used. The Filipinos almost worship the Americans. Sometimes their gratefulness made me feel ashamed. There were buggy drivers also, which we used. We tipped all who served us— over tipped, I'd say. We certainly were not guilty of spreading any ill-will. We leave tomorrow to never return—I hope!

28 May 1945
Subic Bay

I have been off the watches for the past couple of days because I have had a severe headache. I needed a rest also.

Honaker and I are not speaking, which suits me fine. LT Murphy leaves us tomorrow, and Mr. Underhill is the Communications Officer.

Heard from home. Brother Norman is still at home trying to regain his strength. Sure hope I live to see him.

The Philippine Islands

30 May 1945
At sea

We are out for antiaircraft practice with the *Nicholas, Taylor* and *Killen*. Will return to port about 1530. It looks like we are headed back to Leyte to assist in convoy duty. What a pain in the neck! It will be a relief to get away from the monotony of practice, practice, practice! Will probably leave tomorrow.

1 June 1945
At sea

Well, well; the *Burns*, DD588, came alongside and we transferred all of our 7th Fleet data to her. We are on our way to Leyte. I think that is the last time we will see Subic Bay. Guessing again! Manila! That city will be a great liberty port, but it cannot compare with the smallest burg in "Uncle Sugar!"

We will get 10 days alongside a destroyer tender prior to joining the 3rd Fleet. We haven't the latest fighting-ship equipment, although that may not be necessary. Destroyers are being sunk up there around Okinawa regardless of how we are equipped. They may need a little more "Jap bait."

3 June 1945
At sea

We are due in Leyte about noon today. I do hope we immediately go alongside the tender as we have 10 days availability, which will mean 10 days rest for the radiomen because the tender assumes the Fox skeds and other communications. Mr. Underhill and I get along very well. He comes to me for enlightenment instead of the Chief, which surprises me!

4 June 1945
Leyte, San Pedro Bay

Boy! This place really has become quite a naval base. Ships of all descriptions are at anchor. There are eight destroyers here that cannot get underway because of damage they received at Okinawa, which no doubt will become our next battleground. We know we will be in a striking force under the command of "Bull" Halsey. We are alongside the tender *Sienna* for the next 10 days to get ready for the next action. These destroyers here are a mess. "Snuffy" Smith, our former Captain is here. He came over to tell our Captain all the dope, and how he is winning the war. I don't know if his ship is one of those damaged. Most likely.

Yep—we aren't through with the war. The war that we must fight for our country and all that goes with it!

6 June 1945
Leyte

We took over the Fox Sked watch yesterday at noon as the *Nicholas* went into the floating dry dock for a bottom overhaul. No rest for the wicked. We have two more radio units aboard now so we will be able to guard all circuits while up north.

While alongside these other destroyers, we have picked up quite a few "sea stories" and we know what to expect when we get up there. The destroyers that were sunk up there were on "picket patrol." These ships patrol on the outskirts of the fleet. This is the kind of duty we had for the first time, and the destroyer that relieved us was struck by a "dive smasher." If we have to go back to that kind of duty, we will earn it by the sweat of fear and a trustworthy God! And, the rest that we get alongside this tender may have to last us for a long time.

8 June 1945
Leyte

Still alongside the tender *Sienna*. We are still installing new radio equipment to be used around Okinawa. Some of our guys do not feel that we will get back alive. I think God has taken care of us thus far, so He won't stop now! We are really making these days count, taking care of ship's needs.

9 June 1945
Leyte

Haven't done much of anything today, but in the near future, am sure we will have plenty to do. NPM (Major radio circuit) runs at about 26 words per minute now, and after four hours of that, one is awfully tired. (Copying Morse code on a typewriter.) We will be awfully busy when we get to the Okinawa area. I am guessing again, but I am sure that is where we are going. Yep, we have ordered heavy clothing and the covered vents to prepare for rough seas.

Received a note from my girl friend and a note from Aunt Addie, Bill, and Betty. Billy tickles me, it seems that he wants to be called Douglas, Jr., now. I know how he feels. I don't suppose I will ever outlive my nickname "Tot" at home. I wouldn't mind what they called me if I could be at home.

13 June 1945
Leyte

We had to move from alongside the tender to make room for four damaged Tin Cans. Also another carrier, the *Hancock*, all fouled up. These ships that are here that are all fouled up should be in Navy Yards for repairs.

14 June 1945
Leyte

We are getting underway tomorrow for points north to join the 3rd Fleet with Admiral Halsey in Command on the *Missouri*. The Destroyer Division 21; the *Nicholas, Taylor, O'Bannon*, and the cruiser *Oklahoma City*, are to meet outside the harbor.

Read a report today on the suicide attacks. One hundred and eighty-two ships have been damaged, most of them destroyers (My old ship, *William D. Porter*, DD579, was sunk.) Some of the ships were hit two or three times, and 28 of them were sunk—10 of which were destroyers. A DMS was sunk also. It is obvious that every ship we have is needed out here, and that we won't leave until this war is over.

15 June 1945
At sea

We are with the *Taylor*, *Nicholas*, and *Oklahoma City*, and for once I have no inkling as to where the destination is. However, I do know that we are to expect enemy attacks 300 miles from our destination which is Code. DESDIV 21 is going there for duty. The *Oklahoma City* is going there for temporary duty.

We practiced fire at "drones" today (radio-controlled airplanes) and knocked down two of their three. Good shooting! LT(j.g.) Huck and his fire control gang are doing an excellent job!

Still waiting for the news as to where we are going. The *Taylor* picked up our mail before we left and sent it over by whaleboat. Received a "V" mail from my mother. She still thinks I am going to walk in on her. No chance.

(*O'Bannon* rendezvoused with Rear Admiral Litch's escort carrier task group on 17 June off Okinawa.)

18 June
At sea

We have joined a force of six escort carriers, several destroyers and destroyer escorts. Also, the *Oklahoma City* is still with us. Planes are constantly in the air as we are escorting shipping going to Okinawa. We are just below Okinawa on the southeast side.

Noon: We are going in behind each of the carriers and taking aboard an aviator. I don't know why.

20 June 1945
At sea

Still patrolling—up and down—monotonous as hell. This Exec is a pain in the neck! Always a drill—exercising all batteries at GQ. A fella gets tired after a mid-watch, then an early "morning alert" at 0500, then more drills! We are copying two skeds now. Okinawa expeditionary sked, and radio Guam. Both keep us busy.

23 June 1945
En route to Leyte

We expected a good month patrolling with those carriers, but we received orders to Leyte to join another group of carriers.

24 June 1945
En route to Leyte

Holiday routine today, and me with the watch. All is going along smoothly as can be now. I have an extra man on my watch now. A kid from radio school. He runs off at the mouth too much. Outside of that, he can be tolerated. He can copy code, and eases the duty somewhat.

26 June 1945
San Pedro Bay, Leyte, P.I.

Here we are at anchor again. Our orders were changed one day before we came in, which gives us a little longer stay in port. I believe we will be working with escort carriers, which will mean long periods at sea, although it isn't bad duty except for the early "morning alert" at 0500. It is tough after standing a mid-watch. We are tied up with the *Taylor*, and we are splitting the communications duty. Mr. Wiss is driving us crazy with drills

27 June 1945
Leyte

We were all set to secure for about five days tied up alongside the *Taylor* and splitting the communications duty, but fate does not favor us. We have been assigned to Ulithi in the Palais. The *Taylor* will not join us. We leave tomorrow morning. (Ulithi is 360 miles southwest of Guam, 850 miles east of the Philippines, 1300 miles South of Tokyo.)

Yesterday was the ship's birthday. We had a big feed and "happy hour" on the foc's'le (no booze). The "C" Division put on a series of skits. The Captain had a young boy with smooth cheeks sitting next to him, and the Captain had the officers bring him cake and ice cream, water, etc. The Old Man got a kick out of it.

3 July 1945
At sea

We spent a couple of days alongside the *Nicholas* in Ulithi Harbor. It is an island atoll very much like Majuro in the Marshall Islands. The climate is somewhat cooler than the other ports, and I managed to get a couple of good night's sleep because the *Nicholas* took over the radio watches, which gave us some rest.

Our orders for this operation look pretty grim. We are protecting a convoy of tankers that will fuel the front-line ships. We also have a salvage unit, and a Hospital ship that is to take care of casualties, which is believed to be quite a few. We may go in to bombard. We will be off Honshu about 100 to 300 miles throughout the whole show. Oh, yes, we have a couple of escort carriers in the group also. We need the air protection.

4 July 1945
At sea

Another holiday spent on a quiet, beautiful sea. The days are nice, except for the heat. Tomorrow, the raids will start on Tokyo airfields and other areas, then two days later, we will expect the front line ships to come in for fuel. Maybe sooner. Damage to them is also expected.

5 July 1945
At sea

The days are pleasant, and, luckily, there are no enemy planes to mar them. Wiss, the Exec, is still drilling the pants off us, and we are helpless.

6 July 1945
At sea

We are cruising in perfect weather, although it is a little too warm below decks. Task Force 38 fueled from the tankers behind us. It gets light here about 0330. This causes us to rise and shine for the "morning alert."

Leaned that we have a new Communications Officer on the way to join us. Mr. Samuel Goldstein. Wonder what this guy will be like?

10 July 1945
At sea

What a life! We go to "morning alert" at 0320. It is also getting a bit chilly. My blood is like lemonade.

We are supposed to be out here for 30 more days, and even one or two of the officers have stated that we may go back to the States. Baloney! We will be here to the end of this war! We have taken the war to the Japanese, and hopefully this won't go on forever.

Here it is four in the morning and our guys are shooting at a floating mine. We have sunk a few buoys and floating objects on this trip. Some of the mines have exploded, but other than that, the cruise thus far has been uneventful. Just received the news that my old ship, the *William D. Porter,* was sunk by a dive smasher. By the way, we learned from "Tokyo Rose" that the suicide planes are "Kamikazes." We gave them all kinds of names. Our ships and planes are really giving the Japs hell now!

One of the Crew, USS O'Bannon, World War II

11 July 1945
At sea

Aha! It is really getting cold around here. All of us have broken out our sweaters and jackets. We are now only 4500 miles from San Francisco, and a few degrees above its latitude. The closest we have been to the West Coast of the USA in over a year.

Tomorrow we fuel the Task Force 38 striking force, and take off all casualties. The Japanese are really catching hell now. In addition to the carrier strikes, the B-24 Liberators at Okinawa, and the B-29 bombers from Saipan are laying on fire bombs. I don't know how the Japs can continue to resist, but they are a determined people, and I feel that an invasion of Japan proper will have to come to pass.

12 July 1945
At sea

This has been an eventful day so far. Captain Smith's Squadron, our former skipper, had one of its destroyers with engine trouble— the *English*. Capt. Smith spotted the *O'Bannon* and suggested to the boss on the *North Carolina*, that the *O'Bannon* take the place of the *English*, which was approved. We are now assigned to the Tokyo striking force, and we are now on our way to Fujiama with the force of several carriers, destroyers, and battlewagons. Captain Smith sent us greetings. At least it won't be monotonous duty.

Yipe! 20 months out here, and we are finally joining the Navy! Most of the guys are pretty excited. We are assigned to CTG 38.1 and will bombard the coast of Japan. Our equipment is a little out of date, however. The Randolph, a CVL (heavy cruiser), is passing over some new radio equipment. All four boilers are to be used at maximum speed!

(Rendezvoused with Rear Admiral Bogan's Carrier Task Group 38.3 on 12 July 1945.)

CHAPTER 12

JAPAN

Friday, 13 July 1945
At sea

Here we are off the coast of Japan. The little *O'Bannon* groaned under the pace set by the newer ships, but we are hanging right in there. The weather is foul, the sea is rough and cold with a thick fog over the area. This morning, the spotter planes were sent up, but recalled because of the weather. It is now 0500, and they are having trouble getting them back aboard.

This kind of weather is rough on our crew as we have been in a tropical climate for a year and a half, and our blood is thin. Not anything to do when off watch but to hit the sack, and then the movement of the ship makes it hard to sleep.

Admiral Halsey sent over a "well done" to all the ships in the force. Admiral Halsey also passed along congratulations from Admiral Nimitz and Secretary of the Navy Forrestal.

The planes from the carriers were launched for an air strike, but were recalled because of the foul weather. However, we will give them hell tomorrow. Battleships and cruisers will bombard all day tomorrow with their long-range guns, and try and destroy a group of railroad ferries that are in operation. The primary targets of our planes are aircraft, as the number one goal is to wipe out the Nip air force.

We may be assigned to bombard even though we are new in this striking force. Admiral Halsey said in a message, which I read, that the *O'Bannon* was most welcome to join his force anytime.

One of the Crew, USS O'Bannon, World War II

14 July 1945
At sea, 60 miles off the coast of Japan.

Here we are 60 miles off the Nip homeland. The carriers launched all their planes with only one accident. Two men were lost over the side from one of the ships because of the foul weather. As Admiral King says, "men are expendable."

We are steaming along at 27 knots, which makes us bad targets for submarines, and the old *O'Bannon* is holding its own. I am glad we are in the big show. I would not feel right wearing a battle star for escorting fuel tankers. Hope we come out of this okay. We tailed the carriers until all planes landed. We took aboard four crew members of the "Hell Dives." Two were shot down by 40mm guns and two had crashed into the sea because they ran out of gas. One of the radiomen on one of the planes came up to the radio shack. He said there was some AA fire in the harbor by small craft, but no real opposition. Our crew members had dipped one of the plane pilots in the drink as he was being transferred by Boatswain's Chair from destroyer to destroyer, which is quite a shock at 27 knots!

During this operation, we went back past the group behind us which was Admiral Halsey's personal force: three beautiful battleships, the *Iowa*, *Missouri*, and *New Jersey*. Also several of the top, first-line carriers. Quite a sight to see!

Just came on watch to learn that we have been shifted to another Task Group. Task Groups 35.3, 38.3, 38.1, and 38.4 are the striking force groups, so much to our disappointment, we will probably be behind the lines again.

The compartments below deck are really chilly, as we have no heat down there. It reminds me of the days at home, when I was a kid, when I had to get up and build a fire in the fireplace.

16 July 1945
At sea, Off Japan

I have read all the dope on results of the bombing raids. They found a battleship to bomb and blew up 27 railroad locomotives. We are operating with the *North Carolina*, *Bataan*, *Randolph*, *Alabama*, a few cruisers and several destroyers, in addition to Captain Smith's division 124. We are very close to the other two groups, which are just over the horizon with all the "big boys." Plane strikes are continuing in perfect flying weather. Our big battlewagons have joined the heavy cruisers in cruising up and down the beach in search of shipping. They bombarded the shore also. The Japs have to be regretting they started this war!

0700: Just received some disappointing news. We are being detached from the "First Team" as soon as we finish refueling. I wanted us to go in and shoot up the beach along with the other ships. We will be back with the old bunch of tankers again, and the rest of the 3rd Fleet in formation around us. A group of "Limey" fleet will share in the glory of winning the war. They have a couple of battered carriers and a string of dilapidated destroyers so the communique will read: "Allied forces shelled Jap positions on Honshu, etc."

1 August 1945
At sea

Reports tell us that Admiral Halsey has asked to extend our operation for 30 more days. The principal target was Jap aircraft. Admiral Halsey is not satisfied with putting the entire Jap Navy out of commission, and raising hell in all the Jap Islands. That old son of a sea cook is out to kill all the Japs he can. We are to stay out 21 more days.

We are in a very rough sea, and we are steaming along at five knots, which makes it worse. The slightest change in course causes the ship to roll about 30 degrees. It makes sleeping uncomfortable, and it causes a real mess in the mess hall.

165

One of the Crew, USS O'Bannon, World War II

2 August 1945
At sea

Had the mid-watch last night and managed to get some sleep. Did get rolled out for a drill of some kind.

4 August 1945
At sea

The days are ticking away, and the sea is somewhat calmer. We are to be detached on the 12th and head for Ulithi. After that, maybe home. The Japs seem to be licked! They must know that they have no hopes of winning this war! According to the news, the *Indianapolis*, a heavy cruiser, was sunk by two torpedoes delivered by a Jap submarine. The *Indianapolis* was on its way from Guam to Leyte. There were only about 200 survivors. There would have been more if they had not been five days in the drink playing tag with the sharks. She had been sunk for five days before it was known that she had been torpedoed. She was traveling unescorted. When the torpedoes struck, the ship most likely went straight to the bottom. I cannot understand any ship going unescorted.

5 August 1945
At sea

We are headed back up north for the last fueling at sea operation. I hope! It is pleasant weather now and great for sleeping. The 13th of the month, we go back to Ulithi, and then to "Uncle Sugar." Could that be possible???

1700: Task Group 38 is coming in for fuel. There is a mess of mail waiting for us in Ulithi.

7 August 1945
At sea

The news came in a short time ago about the Atomic Bomb, and it caused a great deal of discussion about the ship. One bomb that will do damage equivalent to 2000 B-29 bombers is a lot of explosive!

166

We may wipe out the Japs, but what kind of effect will something like that have in the future? How can something like that ever be controlled? It looks like H.G. Wells prophecies are coming close to becoming true! With power like that in harness, there is practically no electronic invention that won't be able to work.

It looks like we will be home by Christmas after all.

8 August 1945
At sea

Looks like will be in port the 16th and 17th. We have been assigned to go out and send radio traffic again. However, there were only a few messages.

The damage reported caused by the Atomic bomb was four-and-one-half miles, all wiped clean. Japan should surrender now.

It looks like the Navy is going to let a few out. A guy has to be an old man in his thirties to come close to being discharged.

Why don't we get to vote for what we want as the Army did. Oh, no! The Navy has to be the overwhelming ruler, and never give the enlisted man an even break! I have 42 points. Fifty-three are required for discharge. One point for each year of age, and three points for each year of service.

10 August 1945
At sea

Wow!!! Came up for the mid-watch to get the best news that I ever hoped to hear! The Japs will accept the Potsdam peace terms, provided that they can keep their Emperor! Why not? Let them keep him, and we can all go home.

We are to join Task Force 38 for another strike tomorrow, but now that peace in the air, we will probably head for port. It means that Admiral Halsey will have to ask the Emperor if he can ride his white horse through the streets of Tokyo. That Atomic bomb must have blown Nagasaki off the map. Oh, God! let it be true!

11 August 1945
At Sea

We joined the "big boys" this morning, and I used it as an incentive to start a little harmless "scuttlebutt". I told everybody that we are going to escort the *Missouri* into Tokyo Bay with Admiral Halsey to sign the peace terms. Yep, the Nips want to keep their little Emperor, and the Allies will leave him be. It seems that I unconsciously timed my Naval career just right with one month to go. We don't want to count the chickens before they hatch, I hope everything works out. We are still in dangerous waters, and anything can happen.

(Joined Rear Admiral A. W. Radford's Carrier Task Group 38.1 on 11 August 1945.)

12 August 1945
At sea

0500: Learned this morning that we aren't going into port anytime soon. Halsey has decided to stay out here until peace is declared. .He was ordered by CINCPAC (Admiral Nimitz) to steam into Tokyo and Nagasaki with the 3rd Fleet as soon as peace is declared.
Latest reports say that the Allies agreed to let Hirohito stay in power, provided that a commission be provided to dictate to him. I am looking forward to going to Tokyo, but I had much rather go home.

1700: We are with Admiral Halsey's force who is on the *Missouri*. We are going right into Tokyo Bay! I think Halsey chose the *O'Bannon*, *Nicholas*, *Taylor*, and *Buchanan* just for this purpose, as he promised to honor these ships for the battle at Guadalcanal. All of us are still in suspense, but it is surprising how everyone seems to be in such a good humor. The prime questions are: "What's the dope?" "Have the Japs given up yet?"

Yep, we topped off with fuel to steam into Tokyo in force. The battleships, carriers, and heavy cruisers are organizing landing parties. Nimitz is now on his way here in the *New Jersey*. MacArthur too; he won't be left out.

13 August 1945
At sea

Admiral Halsey seems undecided as to what to do. Last night, he called the air strikes on Tokyo on and off twice before he finally decided not to do so. We are just cruising now. Admiral Halsey explained that the orders he received were not plain to him. He assigned the *O'Bannon*, *Nicholas*, and *Taylor* as "Flagship Screen" destroyers, which means that we will escort the *Missouri* right into Tokyo Bay when the Japs surrender!

Every Allied radio is announcing Secretary Burns' answer to Japan's peace terms approximately every 15 minutes. We are getting tired of listening, as we are anxiously waiting for the surrender.

Midnight: We hopped to GQ three times today. Twice because our planes did not turn on their identification equipment, and the 3rd time, our fighters knocked down a twin-engined Jap, which was well out of our gun range.

One of our carriers, as soon as "Condition Red" was declared, opened fire on the first plane she saw and knocked down one of our Corsair fighter planes. The Pilot was picked up, however.

We are still waiting anxiously for the Japanese answer. I haven't been able to sleep at night, nor enjoy a meal, since the news came in. This suspense is wearing me down! All I hear is Talk! Talk! Talk! Halsey ordered all ships to break out our battle colors. We went alongside the *Missouri* to pass a package today. A Marine was on deck drilling a platoon of sailors. God, please let it end!

One of the Crew, USS O'Bannon, World War II

15 August 1945
At sea

0400: News came through on an unofficial channel that Japan had accepted the peace terms. Hirohito spoke to his people and said, "Worse has come to worse, and I demand strict obedience to my rule."

Mr. DeLisle, our paymaster, made the announcement at midnight, and I never got a wink of sleep afterward. Switzerland is supposed to pass the news on to the Allies this morning sometime. They had better hurry, because an air strike has been ordered at dawn. Halsey and a few more admirals of the VIP circuit are discussing the uniforms for the landing.

1700: Peace was announced at 1020 this morning. I was in my bunk, and I felt as calm as Babe Ruth at bat. The boys took the news okay. There was no loud yelling, etc. We all sat around the radio speakers, laughed and talked. Wonderful news! However, Admiral Halsey sent out a message that the Jap officers had not surrendered, and to ensure peace, they should be killed. Preparations are being made for a landing force of all ships. There is a possibility that one of our radio gang will be in the occupation force as they want three first class, one Chief, and three second class; all radiomen from the destroyers. Our Captain requested to "wear the best ribbon in our hair" (Referring to the presidential Citation pennant). Halsey came back, "Affirmative—and stroke her cheek." The *Nicholas* is flying her pennant also.

Admiral Halsey made a speech over our radio this afternoon at 1500, commending all hands for a fine job. He opened his remarks with, "Splice the Main Brace." It was a soul-stirring speech in the words of a real peace-loving, yet fighting man. Almost brought tears to my eyes with gladness.

16 August 1945
At sea

Ah, Me! This peace-time Navy is Killing me!

Japan

The Secretary of the Navy wasted no time in drawing up an ALNAV governing discharges. From what I gather, I don't think it is fair. With just one month to go, I don't think I will ever get out of the Navy!
A Jap submarine came to the surface in the middle our group and surrendered today. It is some consolation to know that they realize their predicament.

Halsey had planes taking pictures of this "historic Task force" all day today.

Vice Admiral Rawlings made a speech to the Third Fleet over the radio today praising Halsey and all of our ships. It was inspiring, but we are waiting for orders to go into Tokyo Bay. Judging by the news, we aren't even in the Third Fleet. Rather, we were left out. Admiral Nimitz gave the names of all the destroyers to the Press Association, and we were not named. What an insult!

The point system went into effect today, and I have four points in excess of what is needed, but I have to wait until my enlistment expires on the 26th of September. About 40 men on our ship are eligible for discharge, and I am the youngest. Civilian life, here I come!

This next month is going to be mighty hard for me. The bold fact that I will be able to go home and change my whole adult life is a strain on my nervous system. I suppose we will hang around here until the peace terms are signed. After that, we will lead the Third Fleet into Tokyo Bay. Halsey has reserved the honor for us. Ah, this Peace-time Navy!

17 August 1945
At sea

Yessir! I am beginning to feel more like a civilian every day. That is all the guys are talking about—Discharge, Discharge, etc. "How many points have you got?" In re-counting. there are only about 20 of us who have the number of points needed, and I am the youngest. It is all too good to be true! I can't sleep well thinking about it. I should have some plans, but I don't. Just to be able to go home suits me.

18 August 1945
At sea

I turned down the opportunity to join the Occupation Force. One radioman second class and one LT(j.g.) were designated from this ship. None of us wanted to go, so the Executive Officer selected McCammack because he came aboard last and has had less time out of the States. I figured it was a choice of going home or staying in Japan, and I will take home any day.
General MacArthur is going to have the troops flown in from Okinawa to participate in the occupation. Destroyers are to be stationed along the coast at 100-mile intervals to act as homing ships. Since we do not have the latest radio and radar equipment, we will not be assigned. A good thing too—I don't trust those Japs who have refused to surrender. We are still to escort the *Missouri* in, as far as I know.

19 August 1945
At sea

The *O'Bannon* flew the four-star flag of Admiral Halsey today for about 30 minutes as we transferred the admiral and his staff from the *Missouri* to the British ship, *Duke of York*, for a conference this afternoon. He really is a snappy old son-of-a-gun, and it is indeed an honor to have him aboard! However, the little errand delayed receiving our mail.

While alongside the *Duke of York*, I have never seen such a "crummy-looking" crew in my life. Their faces and clothing appeared to be dirty. They looked pretty bad, but the ship looked in great shape. We transferred "Mac" (McCammack), the "old man" as we called him, and Mr. Rogers, today with landing force equipment, side arms, etc. The days seem to get longer for me. We are to attend a readjustment lecture tomorrow—those with enough points for discharge.

Japan

20 August 1945
At sea

We are still waiting for the word to proceed to Tokyo Bay. I imagine the minesweepers are busy cleaning out the entrance. MacArthur is going to fly a large part of the occupation forces from Okinawa. Every day draws nearer to my day of FREEDOM. The Navy tries to dress it up by calling it "separation."

I do want to climax my naval career by sailing into Tokyo Bay!

Mr. Mitchell gave us a lecture today on the rights of veterans, to prepare us for the future. It all looks rosy!

22 August
At sea

Had all the planes in the air today in peace-time formation—a beautiful sight to see! It is believed that we will go into Tokyo Bay on the 26th. We can't trust the Japs, so we will be at GQ. We have been assigned an anchorage. The Surrender, or peace terms, will be aboard the *Missouri.*

We transferred Vice Admiral Towers to his flagship as new Commander of Task Force 38. He is Admiral McCain's relief (Senator John McCain's father? John McCain's father and grandfather were both prominent 4-star admirals.) Admiral Towers is really an old man. He looked to me like he had an old-age film over his eyes.

23 August 1945
At sea

All groups of ships have been split up now. The *Nicholas, O'Bannon,* and *Taylor* are escorting Admiral Halsey aboard the *Missouri,* and we are all alone. "The fighting three" are leading the procession. I thought the *Buchanan* was going to take the place of the *Taylor*, but Halsey is sticking to Destroyer Division 21. I do wish the other members of DESDIV 21 could be here with us.

There are only the three of us left. The *Fletcher* is in the Navy Yard for overhaul, and had a few 4-inch holes in her; the *Radford*, *Jenkins*, and *LaValette* all struck mines in the Philippine operations. The *Hopewell* and *Ross* were both damaged by shellfire. The *Ross* struck a mine, and was hit by two Kamikaze planes while in dry dock for repairs, which was at Leyte. The *Hopewell* was struck by four 4-inch shells at Corregidor. The *Nicholas* was also struck by eight 40mm shells at Corregidor. The *O'Bannon* and *Taylor* were unscathed..

24 August 1945
At sea

Our force now is composed of the *Nicholas*, *Taylor*, *O'Bannon*, the *Duke of York*, *Missouri*, and a couple of "Limey" destroyers. We will go into Tokyo Bay day after tomorrow.

There are orders to take over the Jap destroyers and sail them into "rear areas" wherever that is?? States? Underhill has assigned me as senior radioman if this comes to pass. I don't want to go, as I do not want my discharge to be delayed. I didn't hesitate to tell Underhill. The Navy can keep me in for an additional 120 days if my services are needed. A rotten deal!

26 August 1945
At sea

We were all set to meet the Jap admiral and get this signing deal over with. However, MacArthur ordered a 48-hour delay because of a typhoon in the area. It is rough as the dickens right now, and I suppose we are on the edge of it. I am most anxious to get this over with. A month out here can go by pretty fast. I do hope I will not have to go on this boarding party. I do plan to go over Underhill's head to the Exec. However, it will be something to tell my grandkids about. This is our 54th day at sea.

I copied the CINCPAC Press Communique, and the *O'Bannon* has been listed as a member of the Third Fleet. Now the folks at home will know where I am.

Japan

27 August 1945
At sea

We are on our way to meet a Jap ship this morning, for sure. The typhoon that threatened the situation yesterday has headed north, and all seems to be clear. However, we are still in some pretty rough weather. Our best baker caught his hands in a swinging door, breaking his hand just aft of the knuckles and cutting off two fingers. (Just a sideline note.) Admiral Halsey issued an order today to the 3rd Fleet as to how to act with the Jap people. He said not to have any intercourse with them, and treat them impersonally, and act superior. He added that they are treacherous and should not be admitted to society. To lay down the law and use force if necessary to see that it is obeyed. Yep, he is an old Jap hater.

Sagami Wan, Japan

We have pulled into this bay with the *Iowa*, *Missouri*, *George the Fifth*, two British destroyers, the *Nicholas*, *Taylor*, and a Japanese destroyer escort. The Jap tin can met us precisely on time, and the *Nicholas* took off the Japanese emissaries, and transferred them by breeches buoy to the *Missouri*. Then, we proceeded on into this beautiful, spacious bay, with the Third Fleet behind us. We have anchored very close to the beach, which looks like a swell summer resort. There is an island offshore on our starboard side that looks like it was a fort of some kind. The Jap destroyer escort looks pitiful beside our mighty ships. We have been listening to the war correspondents on the radio all day— dramatically describing the negotiations. They gave the *Nicholas* quite a build up!

28 August 1945
Sagami Wan, Japan

Spent the night at anchor without mishap. However, we stayed at GQ until well after sunset. We are due to proceed on into Tokyo Bay this afternoon. We are anchored fairly close to the beach, and with a long glass, we can see people swimming and playing with beach balls.

We are still at anchor basking in pleasant weather. I am on midwatch. We did not darken ship. Halsey sent a message to all ships: "This peace-time X; show all lights possible. Let them know we are here." We did. We were also granted permission to show movies topside. The Exec decided not to have them. That guy has made himself unpopular with the crew.

29 August 1945
Tokyo Bay

The *O'Bannon*, *Nicholas*, and *Taylor* escorted the *Missouri* and *Iowa* into this beautiful bay this morning. While coming in, there was a beached Japanese destroyer on our starboard side, and a severely-damaged, camouflaged battleship, *Nagato*, ahead of us at anchor.

Several ships were sunk at their moorings alongside the docks. Could see the smokestacks in Tokyo off in the distance.

On the way in, we passed several gun emplacements and a little fortress with guns protruding all over it guarding the bay. There are only a few ships at anchor here, all American, including the Jap battleship, which is also American.

There is a great emotional feeling welling up inside me, when I see this. It has been a long, miserable time. So many good things are happening now that I can hardly believe it.

30 August 1945
Tokyo Bay

We got off the patrol duty, and fueled and got provisions from a tanker. We are tuned in on the war correspondents and picking up the latest news as it is made. These guys have a habit of dramatizing everything and laying it on a bit thick. However, what they had to say about the released prisoners of war is really pitiful. More and more ships are entering the bay flying the American and British flags. There is also a Netherlands hospital ship to take aboard the POWs.

Japan

The Nips surrendered the Yokosuka Naval Base today.

Two big Jap subs manned by our guys tied up to one of the sub tenders. Some Japs were still aboard. In a way, I would like to man a Jap destroyer. (A stupid thought!) Rumors continue — Homeward Bound!

31 August 1945
Tokyo Bay

Every day seems to get longer, and so do our watches, due to the fact that our security has been relaxed. Everyone and his brother has a message to send, even if it is to get some "ear time" with some admiral. Congratulations and traditional Navy nonsense seems to be jamming every radio circuit.

We have been assigned to take a submarine-prize crew to man a Jap sub that had surrendered to one of our subs at sea. We are going alongside it now. It is a big son of a gun! We found it carried a plane and had a catapult to launch it. She carried a crew of 200 men with 22 officers.

The Captain was a Division commander and committed suicide last night (hari-kari). We transferred our guys on board and escorted the sub back to Tokyo Bay.

2 September 1945
Tokyo Bay

0400: Too many good things are happening! Our orders came in last night on the mid-watch to report to Puget Sound Navy Yard for an overhaul. I wanted to go to Mare Island, but beggars can't be choosers. Yep—finally it is true! I think we are due there the 13th of the month. All of us are skeptical—"seein' is believing."

We left Tokyo Bay about 1700 (1 Sep).[8] We piped "Anchors Aweigh" over the ship's speaker system, and the Captain yelled, "California, Here I Come!"

We took aboard 89 passengers for the States, and they are sleeping anywhere they can find a space.

When the *Nicholas* and *O'Bannon* were tied up alongside the *Missouri*, Admiral Halsey announced on the *Missouri* speaker system to the *Missouri* crew, to take a look at a pair of "fighting ships." The old boy really likes Destroyer Division 21!

We rendezvoused with a group of other ships going back to the States: the *Essex, Massachusetts, San Diego, San Jacinto, Stembel,* and *Astoria*. We have over 100 passengers aboard now, and they are having a tough time sleeping on a hard deck in rough weather.

I sold all my uniforms except a couple of jerseys, dungarees, and skivvies. I sold them for a good price too.

Before getting underway, Butler and I went aboard the *Missouri* for the official surrender ceremony. It lasted only a few minutes. General MacArthur introduced "Skinny" Wainwright[9] and General Percival[10] as witnesses. The Jap Ambassador, or whatever he is,

---

[8] Because of the International Date Line, you will see the surrender date given variously as 1 September or 2 September.

[9] Jonathan Mayhew Wainwright IV, General, United States Army. After witnessing the Japanese surrender aboard the USS Missouri on September 2, he returned to the Philippines to receive the surrender of the local Japanese commander. A hero's welcome in the US was accompanied by promotion to General and the awarding of the Medal of Honor. (source: Wikipedia)

[10] Lieutenant-General Arthur Ernest Percival, was a British Army officer and a World War I hero. He built a successful military career between the wars but is most noted for his involvement in World War II, when he commanded the British and Commonwealth army during the Battle of Malaya and the subsequent Battle of Singapore. (source: Wikipedia)

had to be shown where to sign. I don't now what we expected—a cat of nine tails would have been in order. Wainwright looked awful. The Japs treated our guys like animals in their prison camps. MacArthur handed out several pens—to officers!

CHAPTER 13

HOME!!!

San Francisco!! Wow! This was like entering a new world!

We all had plenty of money to spend since our confinement aboard ship rather limited our spending. No more Spam! We took advantage of the fine food and entertainment that San Francisco had to offer—making fine food the priority. As I said, No More Spam!

After indulging in the gourmet delights of San Francisco, the Navy provided excellent train accommodations to speed us on our way to Millington (TN) Naval Air Base for discharge. Millington is a small town right outside Memphis.

Memphis just happened to be my hometown. When I arrived in Memphis on a Friday in November 1945, at Grand Central Station, I was a 20-minute taxi ride away from my home in South Memphis. The "powers that be" told me to wait for a bus that would take me to Millington. Debating about whether to go to Millington or South Memphis, based on the fact that I hadn't been home or seen my mother in three years, it was a "no brainer"—I hailed a taxi and took off home.

After a wonderful weekend at home with my family, I reported to Millington Naval Air Base on Monday morning—to be royally chewed out by a Lieutenant Commander for being late. I explained to him that I had not seen my mother for three years—and, then—I asked him what he would have done.

He smiled.

I was promptly discharged after having spent six years of my life with the United States Navy—from age 18 to 24.

Yes, I saw quite a bit of the world. I saw some terrible things that I would not ever want to see again. And, I saw some beautiful things that remain good memories.

CHAPTER 14

QUICK OVERVIEW OF PRIOR SERVICE

Even though I don't want this book to be about me, I've been asked to provide just a bit about my service prior to the *O'Bannon*, so here is a brief summary about other ships that I sailed on after volunteering in September 1939.

Finishing boot camp at Norfolk, Virginia, I spent a few weeks as a mess cook before being transferred to the USS *New York*, a battleship. We proceeded to Guantanamo Bay, Cuba, where we took aboard some Marines for a practice amphibious landing at Culebra, Puerto Rico. We were permitted liberty in Mayagüez and San Juan, Puerto Rico, and Havana, Cuba.[11]

I was transferred to the aircraft carrier USS *Ranger* for another boot cruise for the training of new Navy pilots by experienced Navy pilots. I was a Seaman First Class at this time. I was Bow Hook on the Captain's Gig, which is a 40-foot cabin cruiser. By now, the "winds of war" were blowing fiercely.

Next, I was transferred to the USS *Lang*, DD399, a 1750-ton displacement destroyer at Pearl Harbor. En route to Pearl Harbor, while at Long Beach, California, I was aboard the USS *Arizona*[12] for about two weeks while awaiting transportation to Pearl Harbor aboard the aircraft carrier USS *Saratoga*. The *Saratoga* was taking a load of P-40 aircraft out for General Claire Chennault and his "Flying Tigers" in China.

After arriving aboard the *Lang*, I "struck" to be a radioman. We had a ball in Honolulu—train, train, train—then party, party, party (Liberty) on weekends until midnight of each day—

---

[11] This was many years before Fidel Castro took over Cuba and turned it into the first Communist state in the Western Hemisphere.

[12] The battleship USS *Arizona*, which was sunk by the Japanese at Pearl Harbor on 7 December 1941, now serves as a memorial representing all who lost their lives that day. The USS *Arizona* Memorial is built over the wreckage in Pearl Harbor—the final resting place for 1,102 of her crew.

swimming on Waikiki Beach—girls, girls, girls—hot baths and massages—Luaus—booze. In spite of all the partying, I did manage to learn Morse code and was promoted to Radioman Third Class.

The "winds of war" continued to blow—stronger and stronger.

Many new ships were being commissioned and radiomen were in great demand. After receiving my radioman rating, I was transferred to the USS *Pokomoke*, which was then being commissioned and fitted out for duty at the Portsmouth Navy Yard, across the James River from Norfolk.

I left Honolulu in May 1941.

§§§

USS *Pokomoke*

One ship was the USS *Pokomoke*, AV9, a seaplane tender.

This was prior to the United States' entry into World War II. I believe this was in early 1941.

We were involved in the "undeclared war in the North Atlantic," stationed in Argentia, Newfoundland. Our seaplanes, PBYs and PBMs, using radar, would go out and spot German submarines. The subs were really taking a toll of the lend-lease ships, which were going to England. When our planes spotted a sub, British, French, Belgian and Polish crews aboard Corvettes (a small sub-chaser type vessel) loaded with depth charges would go out and try to sink the subs. It was a successful operation.

I attended one of the first radar schools, using British radar equipment, during this tour of duty.

One incident stands out most clearly in my memories of the Pokomoke. I was on the new radar equipment that had been installed aboard the Pokomoke. My radar screen was filled with a solid mass of fluctuations, and I thought it was land.

The commander of Patrol Wing Seven, who outranked our captain, ordered, "Commence Firing!"

Our captain ordered, "Belay that order!"

As it turned out, we were in the middle of a huge convoy of lend-lease ships on their way to England. It was fortunate that "cooler heads prevailed." It was the dead of night, and we could not see beans. We finally had to turn on our running lights to avoid running into the ships of the convoy.

The *Pokomoke* served as a "flag" ship; a communications ship for all ships in the Argentia, Newfoundland area. We handled communications and radar for the British, Polish, Belgian and French ships. Radiomen were also Radar men in those early days of radar. (After the rating of Radarman was created, I had the choice to be either a Radarman or a Radioman. I chose Radioman.)

At a later date, my captain recommended me to become a Navy pilot. Because of a deviated septum (acquired during my high school boxing days), I was transferred to the Navy Hospital in Chelsea, Massachusetts, for repair. After being released from the hospital and in the receiving station at Boston Navy Yard, I lost interest in becoming a pilot. The brass pulled me out of the receiving station and made me a supervisor of the watch at Boston Navy Yard.

At that time, draftees were pouring into the Navy, and ships were being built at a record pace. Radiomen who were qualified to stand a watch were hard to come by and very much in demand. Because of my duty aboard the Pokomoke, I was qualified to supervise watches on any ship. Radiomen aboard the ships that were being repaired stood the watches, and I supervised one of the watches. I had eight hours on and thirty-two hours off. Most radiomen would kill for that kind of duty! A LT Ryan told me I could stay there for the duration of the war, but, foolish me, I wanted "some action!"

One of the Crew, USS O'Bannon, World War II

USS *William D. Porter*

I got transferred to new construction to put a destroyer in commission in Orange, Texas, in 1943. This was the *William D. Porter*, DD579. We took our "shakedown" cruise in the Caribbean.

The Porter was known as an unlucky ship—with good reason. Beginning with her maiden voyage, as she backed out of the dock at Norfolk and struck a sister ship, she was to have many, many accidents during her "unlucky" career.

We lost one guy over the side during some rough weather, and he was never found. He was a newly-rated radio technician. It was written up by the *Miami Herald* newspaper as a sensational incident. After the war, *Sea Classics Magazine* interviewed me for another article on this subject.

In another unlucky incident—that could have been horribly disastrous—the *"Willie D"* accidentally fired a live torpedo at the USS *Iowa*, with President Franklin D. Roosevelt aboard, on his way to a conference in Tehran, Iran, to meet with Stalin and Churchill! Also aboard were Secretary of State Cordell Hull and all the World War II top brass. (Just before this, we had lost a depth charge overboard and created an explosion that was scary and embarrassing.)

The ship was put under arrest, and we remained at a dock in Bermuda for about two weeks. It was the first time that a complete ship's company had been arrested in the history of the US Navy. Each and every man was questioned by the Office of Naval Intelligence (ONI); some men more than once. As a result, every torpedoman was reduced in rank, including the Torpedo Officer, and transferred throughout the fleet. It was the end of his naval career for the commanding officer.

The Navy, understandably, kept a lid on this incident until many years after the war was over and President Roosevelt was long dead.

Afterwards, we supported the landings in the Aleutian Islands—Adak and Attu. From there, we went to Pearl Harbor in late 1944, and it was here that I was transferred to the USS *O'Bannon*.

After several more unfortunate accidents, the William D. Porter was sunk by a Kamikaze plane at Okinawa in 1945.

EPILOGUE

My six years in the Navy were crucial in that I had the opportunity to observe and learn from others. The close confinement of a ship brings out the best and the worst in men. I was able to see and analyze how both officers and enlisted men reacted to stress and to fear. I was able to observe the intelligence of men as compared to their education. I was able to observe the character of both officers and enlisted men. I learned how to get along with people and to not let any disagreements with their ways of acting affect me too much. I was able to compare my own abilities with those of the officers and enlisted men that I was living and working with, and to see that I had abilities and potential.

All of this brought me to the realization that, in spite of the hardships I had endured growing up poor in Memphis, Tennessee, it was up to me to use the intelligence and character that I had to make my own future opportunities in the world. By now, I had matured to the point where I knew that I was ready to accept the challenge of moving on in the world. I realized that by hard work and persistence, I would be able to overcome obstacles and accomplish much. Perhaps you might wonder why I felt that I had obstacles to overcome.

A Little Background of My Life Before the US Navy

A bit of my pre-Navy background: I was born on 25 July 1921, and grew up on the south side of Memphis during the Great Depression. My mother had four sons to raise alone. We were poor. It was a blow to my ego to be going to high school with holes in my shoes, ragged seats in my pants, and fried egg sandwiches or "pressed chicken" (bologna) for lunch. We didn't have all the government welfare programs then that exist now. If we had, I'm sure my family would have qualified.

To help support the family, I had an after-school paper route delivering the afternoon paper, *Memphis Press Scimitar*, to several professional buildings downtown. In addition, I sold

Epilogue

magazines such as *The Ladies Home Journal*, *Liberty*, and the *Saturday Evening Post* door-to-door.

After graduating from high school, things weren't much better. The best job I could get was as an errand boy for Western Union making $12 per week, plus the dime tips. Holmes Bicycle Shop, where I did weekend odd jobs for Mr. Holmes, sold me a used bicycle for no money down and fifty cents a week, which allowed me to take the Western Union job.

In addition to that, I had a side job as a pin boy in a duck-pin bowling alley, and across the street at Tom Rigger's Pool Room, I was a "rack boy."

While working at Tom Rigger's, I learned to shoot a pretty good game of pool. In fact, Tom let me shoot "house stick." When an opponent beat me, he got to play free; when I won, he had to pay. Sometimes Tom would bet on me. It was good for my ego.

However, I eventually decided to join the Navy to see if I could improve my prospects in this world.

So much for background...

Back home in Memphis, I got a job as Playground Director for the Memphis Park Commission. In this capacity, I met a young lady who persuaded me to attend the University of Tennessee on the GI Bill[13]. Here I was—24 years old and a freshman! But, I wasn't the only "old" veteran taking advantage of the government's tuition assistance, so I didn't suffer too much.

After two years in the School of Journalism, a reporter on the staff of "Orange and White", the university newspaper, and a pledge to the Sigma Phi Epsilon fraternity, I realized that I could not continue to live in a fraternity house on $108 per month. I needed a job with an opportunity. Even though the two years at UT had been beneficial in supplementing my education and adding to my maturity, I felt it was time to move on. By now, I had gained great confidence in my ability to do whatever I set my mind to. I wasn't just looking for a job— I was looking for an opportunity!!

---

[13] GI Bill – a veterans education benefit program of the US government

I returned to Memphis and applied for a job with L. M. Berry & Co., which handled all the yellow-page advertising sales for Southern Bell Telephone Company in Atlanta. At that time, there was only one "Yellow Pages"—**The** "Yellow Pages."

I considered myself an excellent salesman—still do. During my three-and-a-half years with the Berry Company, I met my Rosalie. We were married in New Orleans, Louisiana, in January 1950. (We recently celebrated our 56th anniversary!)

We both realized that we could not continue to live out of suitcases in hotels; we wanted to raise a family. So, we moved to Memphis where I became a distributor/salesman for major home appliances and televisions. (Television was still in its infancy then.) I was successful, but still wasn't earning enough money to support a family. After all, my first year with "Yellow Pages," as a single man, I had earned more than $18,000. That was a lot of money in 1948.

By now, that family that Rosalie wanted was coming along nicely. Our first child was a daughter, Susan, born in 1953, followed by Timothy in 1956. Son Jeffrey came along a little later, in 1962.

Bob Thompson, a former manager for L. M. Berry & Co., who became manager for Allstate Insurance Company, contacted me, and to make a long story short, I became an Allstate Insurance agent in Memphis. After a year and a half, I opened my own Casualty Insurance Agency, "Walter Lee Insurance Agency," in Memphis. After eleven successful years, I sold the agency. I had become a real estate affiliate broker while operating the agency, and had sold a couple of houses on the side.

A friend of mine was with Fairfield Communities, Inc., out of Arkansas, a resort real-estate developer. In 1971, he convinced me that I should join him at Fairfield Glade, Tennessee, one of their developments. I enjoyed working there for several years, finally "buying what I sold" and retiring here with my Rosalie.

PHOTOGRAPHS

USS *O'BANNON* (DD250)

One of the Crew, USS O'Bannon, World War II

"C" Division (Communications Division),
USS *O'BANNON*
(Walter Lee, sitting, second person on the right)

One of the Crew, USS O'Bannon, World War II

Crew of the USS *O'Bannon*

One of the Crew, USS O'Bannon, World War II

Officers of the USS *O'Bannon*, 1944

One of the Crew, USS O'Bannon, World War II

Captain Alfred Pridmore

Captain Donald J. MacDonald

One of the Crew, USS O'Bannon, World War II

USS *O'Bannon* Officers

Sherrif (Signalman)

Natives in Leyte, the Philippines

One of the Crew, USS O'Bannon, World War II

USS *O'Bannon*
Followed by the USS *Jenkins* and USS *Taylor*

Grande Island, Subic Bay, the Philippine Islands

One of the Crew, USS O'Bannon, World War II

```
NR S 5576  -O-  -A-  2SX  271725/1  Z4A  GR 24  BT

    ENEMY CONVOY 1 BB 1 CA 4 DD SIGHTED 1600/1 BEARING 270 DEGREES
    *** DISTANCE 225 MILES FROM SAN JOSE COURSE 140 DEG...BT

                                TOR/0945/BOYTE/FOXSKEDS/27 DEC....

FROM:- RECCO PLANE:
   TO:- AUICO SOWESTPACFOR                    WU/LEE
```
We were at San Jose when this came in!

URGENT

Typical messages received by the *O'Bannon*
Communications Division

```
NR O 945 -O--A-  LL4E7  050015  LM5M  LK9P  GR 23 BT

    UNDER AERIAL TORPEDO ATTACK X TWO SHIPS HIT X REQUEST COVER POSITION
    LAT NINE FIFTY TWO NORTH LONG ONE TWO SEVEN SEVENTEEN EAST

                                TOR/LEE/0523// 5 DEC...

FROM:- CTU 78.4.7:
   TO:- CTF 75 / CTF 76...
```
FROM: COMMANDER TASK UNIT 78.4.7

One of the Crew, USS O'Bannon, World War II

U.S.S. O'BANNON DD 450

NR D 330 NR S 3723 -O-F-A- HOW2 242227 5GCY -W- CRU3 THOS
WVP2 Z2NP BT

ENEMY FORCE ATTACKING OUR CVES COMPOSED OF FOUR BATTLESHIPS EIGHT
CRUISERS AND OTHER SHIPS X REQUEST LEE PROCEED AT TOP SPEED FOR
LEYTE X REQUEST IMMEDIATE STRIKE BY FAST CARRIERS.

SYSTEM: TOR/25 OCTOBER

FROM: CTF 77

ACTION TO: COM 3RD FLEET.

INFO TO: ALL TASKFORCE COMMANDERS 7TH FLEET/ ALL TASKFORCE COMMANDERS 3RD FLT.

One of the Crew, USS O'Bannon, World War II

Joe Pot Jivers

One of the Crew, USS O'Bannon, World War II

Joe Pot Jivers, Happy Hour

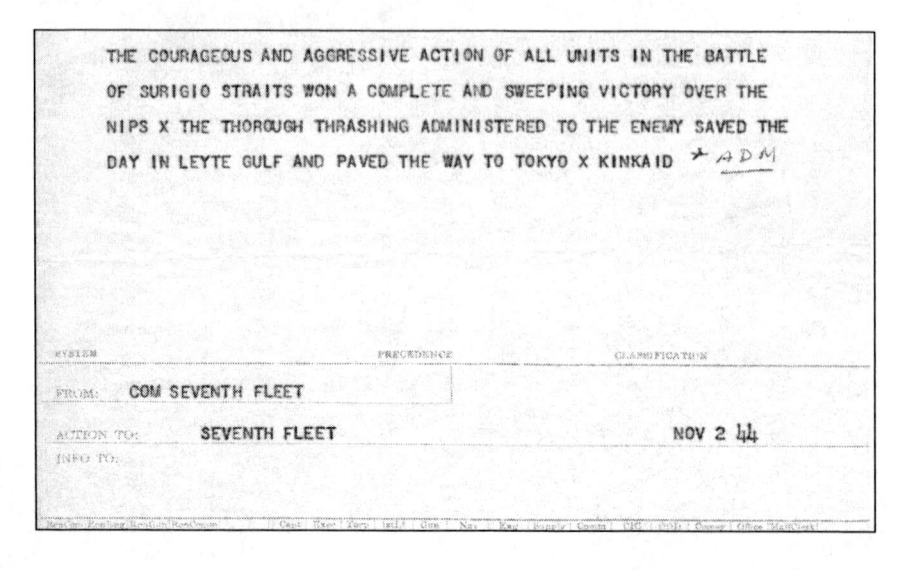

THE COURAGEOUS AND AGGRESSIVE ACTION OF ALL UNITS IN THE BATTLE OF SURIGIO STRAITS WON A COMPLETE AND SWEEPING VICTORY OVER THE NIPS X THE THOROUGH THRASHING ADMINISTERED TO THE ENEMY SAVED THE DAY IN LEYTE GULF AND PAVED THE WAY TO TOKYO X KINKAID

FROM: COM SEVENTH FLEET
ACTION TO: SEVENTH FLEET   NOV 2 44
INFO TO:

One of the Crew, USS O'Bannon, World War II

```
THE SECRETARY OF THE NAVY SAYS THE THIRD FLEET HAS DONE IT AGAIN AND
I PASS ON TO YOU ALL HIS CONGRATULATIONS AND THE NATIONAL AND
PERSONAL PRIDE SO WARMLY EXPRESSED IN HIS MESSAGE X HALSEY

FROM: COM THIRD FLEET
ACTION TO: THIRD FLEET                                    NOV 3 54
```

Congratulations from Admiral Halsey

One of the Crew, USS O'Bannon, World War II

Congratulations from Admiral Halsey

O'BANNON (DD450)

120000 GR 37 BT

SECNAV HAS GIVEN THE 3RD FLEET A WELL DONE AND CINCPAC ADDS
HIS OWN CONGRATULATIONS FOR STRIKE ON JAPAN X IT IS A PLEASURE
TO PASS IT ON TO THE MEN WHO DID THE JOB X HALSEY

TOR/0437/HUDSON/FL/13 JULY (FRIDAY)   WU/LEE

FM:- COMPACFLT
TO:- TASKFORCE 38 / COM 3RD FLEET

CLEARED

One of the Crew, USS O'Bannon, World War II

```
                      U.S.S. O'BANNON (DD450)

TBS TRANSMISSION            TOR/1924

X WELL DONE TO ALL HANDS IN TG 30.8 FOR TOSSING MORE BEANS X BULLETS
AND BUG JUICE THAN HAS EVER BEEN DONE BEFORE X YOUR UNTIRING EFFORTS
HAS ONLY BEEN EQUALLED BY THOSE IN TF 38 WHO RECEIVED WITH ENTHUSIASM
EVERYTHING THAT YOU COULD PITCH X THIS BIG BLUE TEAM COULD NOT POSSIB
LY CONTINUE WITHOUT MORE WELL PLANNED AND STRENUOUS SUPPORT FOR EVERY
BOMB AND BULLET THAT WE HAVE BEEN ABLE TO DROP ON THE NIPS X SIGNED
HALSEY


TOR/1924/COMBAT/TBS/22 JULY                              WU/LEE

FROM:- CTG 30.8
  TO:- TG 30.8
```

Our task group detached to escort carriers on Kurils raid 12 July rejoined 17 July. detached again; special mission as radio deception ship 21 July cruised just off Tokyo rejoined 22 July.

A "Well Done" from Admiral Halsey

One of the Crew, USS O'Bannon, World War II

> **Heading:**
>
> PROUDLY I SEND THIS PARTING WELL DONE TO MY VICTORIOUS ALL – SERVICES SOUTH PACIFIC FIGHTING TEAMS. YOU MEN HAVE, MEASURED, AND MOWED DOWN THE BEST THE ENEMY HAD ON LAND AND SEA AND IN THE AIR. YOU HAVE SENT HUNDREDS OF TOJOS SHIPS, THOUSANDS OF HIS PLANES, TENS OF THOUSANDS OF HIS SLIPPERY MINIONS WHENCE THEY CAN NEVER AGAIN ATTACK OUR FLAG,
>
> NOR THE FLAGS OF OUR ALLIES. YOU BEAT THE JAP IN THE GRIM VICTORY AT GUADALCANAL; YOU DROVE HIM BACK AND HUNTED HIM OUT; YOU BROKE HIS OFFENSIVE SPIRIT IN THOSE SMASHING BOUGAINVILLE – RABAUL BLOWS AT HIS SHIPS AND PLANES AND TROOPS IN NOVEMBER 1943; AND YOU SMEARED HIM AND ROLLED OVER HIM TO EASILY OCCUPY EMIRAU. AND NOW, CARRY ON THE SMASHING
>
> SOUTH PACIFIC TRADITION UNDER YOUR NEW COMMANDERS, AND MAY WE JOIN UP AGAIN FARTHER ALONG THE ROAD TO TOKYO.
>
> HALSEY
>
> THIS IS AN UNCLASSIFIED DISPATCH AND MAY BE COPIED
>
> From: ADMIRAL HALSEY
> Action To: ALL HANDS, SOUTH PACIFIC....

From Admiral William Halsey upon his departure

One of the Crew, USS O'Bannon, World War II

```
142052 GR 69 BT

THE NIP OFFICERS ARE STILL FIGHTING X THAT MEANS WE ARE STILL
FACING AN ENEMY THAT HATES OUR CARRIERS LIKE THE DEVIL HATES
HOLY WATER X UNTIL THE NIPS SURRENDER AND ARE DISARMED RPT DIS-
ARMED THEY ARE DANGEROUS AND NEED KILLING X THE BEST PRESENT
INSURANCE FOR OUR FORCES AND FUTURE INSURANCE FOR PEACE IS TO
CARRY IT TO THEM WITH EVERYTHING WE HAVE X CARRY ON X HALSEY


WU/BUTLER/0030/15 AUG 45...

FROM:- COM THIRD FLEET
   TO:- TASK FORCE 38
```

From Admiral Halsey
after the Atomic Bomb dropped

> Form No. 95   U.S.S. O'BANNON (DD450)
>
> -A- D450   150255   0F3   GR 11 BT
>
> O'BANNON REQUESTS PERMISSION TO WEAR HER BEST RIBBON IN HER HAIR
>
> BT YOUR 150255 AFFIRMATIVE X ALSO STROKE HER CHEEK
>
> PRES. UNIT CITATION PENNANT
>
> TOR/VIS/SHERRIF/15 AUG 1945...   WU/LEE
>
> COM THIRD FLEET
>
> O'BANNON (DD450)

Response to Admiral Halsey's message above
(Her "best ribbon" was the Presidential Unit Citation)

One of the Crew, USS O'Bannon, World War II

```
150145 GR 36 BT

TO EVERY OFFICER AND MAN IN THIS SPLENDID GROUP WELL DONE
X IN THE LAST FORTY FIVE DAYS YOU HAVE CONTRIBUTED MUCH
TOWARD THE VICTORY ANNOUNCED TODAY AND I AM PROUD OF YOU X
SIGNED RADFORD

ADM

TOR/1408/VIS/15 AUG 1945                              WU/JC

FROM:- CTG 38.4
  TO:- TG 38.4
```

Congratulations from
Admiral Arthur William Radford

One of the Crew, USS O'Bannon, World War II

Walter Lee, 4 April 1945, in front of Santo Thomas Church, Manila, Philippine Islands

One of the Crew, USS O'Bannon, World War II

One of the Crew, USS O'Bannon, World War II

Tokyo Bay, Sept 1945

One of the Crew, USS O'Bannon, World War II

Tokyo Bay, September 1945

One of the Crew, USS O'Bannon, World War II

Tokyo Bay, September 1945

One of the Crew, USS O'Bannon, World War II

Torpedomen, Tokyo Bay, 1945
(USS Nicholas in background)

One of the Crew, USS O'Bannon, World War II

San Francisco, September 1945
L to R, Harry "Pete" Peterson, Bob "Brownie" Brown,
Walter A. Lee, "Weasel" Johnson

One of the Crew, USS O'Bannon,
World War II
Walter Allen Lee

GEOGRAPHY

I will attempt to indicate the country or location of places referred to in my diary. Some of the names have changed since World War II. Also, some places formerly owned or under the aegis of other nations may now be independent.

Some of the locations and definitions were obtained from Wikipedia, the Free Encyclopedia. Some were obtained from the Merriam-Webster Unabridged Dictionary.

A

Aitape - New Guinea

Argentia - a community on the island of Newfoundland in the Canadian province of Newfoundland and Labrador

B

Bataan – a province of the Philippines occupying the whole of *Bataan Peninsula* on Luzon. The province is part of the Central Luzon region. The capital of Bataan is Balanga City and is bordered by the provinces of Zambales and Pampanga to the north. The peninsula faces South China Sea to the west and encloses its arm, Manila Bay, to the east.[14]

Bicol Region or Bicolandi - one of the 16 regions of the Philippines occupying the Bicol Peninsula at the southeastern end of Luzon Island

---

[14] Wikipedia

Bougainville - Papua New Guinea

C

Caraboa – island in the Philippines

Cebu – island in the Philippines

Celebes – now Sulawesi - a large island in Indonesia. It is the world's eleventh-largest island, covering an area of 174,600 km. The island is surrounded on the west by Borneo, the north by the Philippines, east by Maluku (Malucca, Molucca), and to the south by Flores and Timor.[15]

China Sea - The South China Sea is a marginal sea, part of the Pacific Ocean, encompassing an area from Singapore to the Strait of Taiwan of around 3,500,000 km. It is the largest sea body after the five oceans.[16]

Corregidor - an island in the entrance of the Philippines' Manila Bay

D

Dutch East Indies - Indonesia

E

El Fraile Island (Fort Drum), a heavily fortified island fortress situated at the mouth of Manila Bay in the Philippines, due south of Corregidor Island.

F

Finschhafen – in New Guinea

---

[15] Ibid
[16] Ibid

Fort Drum (El Fraile Island), a heavily fortified island fortress situated at the mouth of Manila Bay in the Philippines, due south of Corregidor Island.

G

Grande Island – at the entrance of Subic Bay, Philippines

Guadalcanal – a province of the Solomon Islands in the Pacific Ocean. Honiara, the capital of the Solomon Islands is here.

H

Halmahera – aka Jailolo, Djailolo, or Gilolo - Island, c.7,000 sq mi (18,100 sq km), East Indonesia, between New Guinea and Sulawesi (formerly Celebes), on the equator. The largest of the Moluccas. (Dutch East Indies is now Indonesia.)[17]

Hollandia - New Guinea

Humboldt Bay – Hollandia, New Guinea

K

Koli Point – Guadalcanal, Solomon Islands

Kriles – in the Pacific Ocean (cannot find anything on this)

L

Leyte Gulf - the Philippines

Lingayen Gulf - an extension of the South China Sea on Luzon in the Philippines

---

[17] Ibid

M

Majuro Bay, Majuro Atoll – Marshall Islands (Micronesia)

Manila Bay/Manila – Manila is the capital of the Philippine Islands

Manus Island - Admiralty Islands, Papua New Guinea

Merah – New Guinea

Milne Bay – New Guinea

Mindanao - the second largest and easternmost island in the Philippines and one of the three island groups in the country, with Luzon and Visavas being the other two [18]

Mindoro - the seventh-largest island in the Philippines. It is located in southwestern Luzon, just northeast of Palawan. Less than 100 miles from Manila

Morotai Island – Molucco or Molucca Group, Dutch East Indies

N

New Caledonia - Oceania, islands in the South Pacific Ocean, east of Australia (between Australia and Fiji); settled by the French [19]

New Guinea - located just north of Australia, is the world's second largest island, having become separated from the Australian mainland when the area now known as the Torres Strait flooded around 5000 BC. The name Papua has also been long-associated with the island. The western half of the island contains the Indonesian provinces of Papua and West Irian Jaya, while the eastern half forms the independent country of Papua New Guinea. [20]

---

[18] Ibid
[19] Ibid
[20] Ibid

New Hebrides – Vanuatu, South Pacific

New Ireland – Papua New Guinea

Noumea - New Caledonia

O

Okinawa – largest island in the Ryukyu Islands, south of the four big islands of Japan

Ormoc Bay – in the Camotes Sea in the Philippine Islands, other side of Leyte

P

Palawan –an island province of the Philippines located in the Western Visayas region. Its capital is Puerto Princesa City and it is the largest province in terms of land area. The islands of Palawan stretches from Mindoro to Borneo in the southwest. It lies between the South China Sea in the northwest and Sulu Sea in the southeast.[21]

Pearl Harbor – in Honolulu, Oahu, Hawaiian Islands

Purvis Bay - Tulagi, Florida Island Group, Solomon Islands

S

Sagami Wan – in Japan. Sagami Wan Bay and Tokyo Bay are where the U S Navy fleet entered the Japanese waters on 27 August 1945 to accept the surrender (Mount Fujiyama is visible from Sagami Wan Bay and Tokyo Bay.)

San Pedro Bay – Leyte, the Philippines

---

[21] Ibid

Sansapor - on the northern coast of New Guinea

Seaddler Harbor – Admiralty Islands (Manus Islands, Papua New Guinea)

Surigao – Mindanao, Philippine Island

Solomon Islands - a nation in the South Pacific Ocean, east of Papua New Guinea, and is part of the Commonwealth of Nations. It consists of more than 990 islands, which together cover a land mass of 28,400 square kilometres.[22]

Subic Bay – a bay on the west coast of the island of Luzon in the Philippines, about 100km northwest of Manila Bay

Sudet - New Guinea

Sulu Sea - situated between Borneo, Palawan and the Philippines

T

Tacloban – capital city of Leyte, the Philippines

Tanah or Tannahmerah/Tanah Merah– New Guinea

Tarakan - Borneo

Ternate - a 4th class municipality in the province of Cavite, Philippines

Tokyo – capital of Japan

Tokyo Bay - a bay in the southern Kanto region of Japan, surrounded by the Boso Peninsula (Chiba Prefecture) and the Miura Peninsula (Kanagawa Prefecture). The ports of Tokyo, Chiba, Kawasaki, Yokohama, and Yokosuka are all located on Tokyo Bay.

---

[22] Ibid

Towi Towi – island group in the Philippines

Treasury Island - Solomon Islands, off the coast of Bougainville

Truk - Chuuk is an island group that comprises one of the four states of the Federated States of Micronesia (FSM). It lies in the Western Pacific Ocean approximately 1000 KM southeast of Guam. Chuuk means *mountain* in the Chuukese language and was known mainly by its German mispronunciation, Truk, until 1990.[23]

Tulagi – Solomon Islands, North of Guadalcanal, part of the Florida Island Group

W

Wewak – Papua New Guinea

Wotje Atoll – an atoll of 75 islands in the Pacific Ocean. A legislative district of the Marshall Islands (Micronesia)

Z

Zamboanga Bay – in Mindanao, Philippine Islands

---

[23] Ibid

GLOSSARY

A

APD – ship that transports troops; high speed transport

B

Boot camp – a station for basic training of newly enlisted seamen

Bow hook – a person on a "gig" or a motor launch who ties up the bow when docking. (The "tail hook" secures the rear end.)

C

CDD – Commander, Destroyer Division

CL – Light Carrier or "Jeep" Carrier

CVL – Heavy cruiser

Condition Able – Stay at Alert. Maintain water-tight integrity; all hatches dogged down, but GQ was relaxed.

Corvette - a fast, lightly-armed warship, smaller than a destroyer, often armed for antisubmarine operations[24]

D

DE – Destroyer Escort

DMS – Destroyer Mine Sweeper

Dog Day – Dog Circuit. A radio circuit that is manned 24 hours each day. We also had "Dog" Day for landings—the equivalent of "D" Day (best I can remember).

---

[24] Answers.com

Glossary

E

Ear banger – brown noser

F

Fathometer – used for a sonic depth finder[25]

Five-star admiral - The five-star general/admiral rank was created in the midst of World War II to address the fact that several American commanders found themselves in the delicate position of supervising Allied officers of higher rank. For the Army, they were known as "General of the Army," and for the Navy, they were known as "Fleet Admiral." When General of the Army Omar N. Bradley died in April of 1981, the five-star ranking was consigned to history. In all, four Army generals, four Navy admirals, and one Air Force general have held this rank. The Army's five star generals were General George C. Marshall, General Douglas A. MacArthur, General Dwight D. Eisenhower, and General Omar N. Bradley. The Navy's five-star fleet admirals were Admiral William D. Leahy, Admiral Ernest J. King, Admiral Chester Nimitz, and Admiral William F. "Bull" Halsey. And General Henry Arnold was the Air Force's five-star general. Who beats a five-star general? A General of the Armies of the United States -- the highest military rank of all time, hands down. To date, only George Washington and John J. Pershing have held this position.[26]

Flash Red – Danger, probable attack

Flash White – All Clear

Flash Yellow – Possible attack, caution, remain at GQ

Fo'c'sle – Forecastle deck

---

[25] Merriam-Webster Unabridged Dictionary
[26] "Ask Yahoo" (modified)

Fox Skeds – a continuous flow of radio traffic, mostly in code, to all ships and navy stations around the world. Transmission are 24 hours per day.

G

General Quarters, GQ – the highest condition of alert on board ship, which pulls the crew from their normal work assignments to a war-fighting stance

GI – Government Issue

H

H-hour – the hour to begin a landing

J

Jeep Carrier – The Navy's escort carriers, called "Jeep carriers," did the routine patrol work, scouting and escorting of convoys that their larger fleet-type counterparts couldn't do. Lightly armored and slower than the fleet carriers and with far less defensive armament and aircraft. Jeep carrier crews, who joked that "CVE" (the Navy's designation for this type of ship) really stood for "Combustible, Vulnerable and Expendable," became experts at hunting, finding and killing U-boats in both ocean theaters. Jeeps and their crews also provided fighter and close air support for amphibious landings, and served as aircraft transports as the tempo of the carrier war in the Pacific mounted to a crescendo.[27]

---

[27] "The Carriers: A Brief History of the U S Navy Aircraft Carriers, the Escort Carriers," researched and written by CE1 Robert A. Germinsky, U.S. Naval Reserve (modified)

Glossary

K

Kamikaze – a member of the Japanese Air Force assigned to make a suicidal crash on a target (or one who volunteers). Also, an airplane containing explosives to be flown into a target. The word is Japanese: Kami = god or spirit; Kaze = wind.

L

LCI – Landing Craft Infantry

LSM – Landing Ship Medium

LST – Landing Ship Tanks

Landing – ships would bombard Japanese positions prior to landing troops

Lend-lease ships – ships built by the Unites States, who had not yet entered the war, then leased or loaned to Great Britain. See Liberty ships.

Liberty ship – Kaiser Frasier (aka Kaiser Frazer) built these quickly during the war for transporting supplies — thus, a supply ship, cheaply made. According to Wikipedia, the Liberty ships were cargo ships built in the United States during World War II. They were cheap and quick to build, and came to symbolize US wartime industrial output. Based on vessels ordered by Britain to replace ships torpedoed by German U-boats, they were purchased for the US fleet and for lend-lease provision to Britain. Sixteen American shipyards built 2,751 Liberties between 1941 and 1945, easily the largest number of ships produced to a single design.

M

Main brace – the brace attached to a ship's main yard[28]

---

[28] Merriam Webster Unabridged Dictionary

Mimeograph machine – a duplicator for making copies that consists of a frame in which the stencil is stretched and an inking roller for pressing ink through the porous lines of the stencil onto paper[29]

Morse code – code in which letters of the alphabet, numbers and other symbols are represented by dots and dashes or long and short sounds and used for transmitting messages by audible or visual signals (as by telegraphy, wigwags, or light flashes)[30]

N

New Deal – various legislation involving government-funded projects pushed by President Franklin D. Roosevelt to solve problems of the Great Depression

NPM – major radio circuit

O

ONI – Office of Naval Intelligence

P

PBM – see PBY

PBY – Patrol Bomber. These were patrol flying boats. The "Y" stood for the manufacturer; in this case, Consolidated Aircraft Company. "M" stood for Martin; the Glenn L. Martin Company. They were used for anti-submarine warfare, air-sea rescue and as a transport.

Presidential Unit Citation – The Presidential Unit Citation is awarded in the name of the President to units of the Armed Forces of the United States and cobelligerent nations for extraordinary

---

[29] Ibid
[30] Ibid

heroism in action against an armed enemy. The unit must have accomplished its mission under such extremely difficult and hazardous conditions as to set it apart from and above other units participating in the same campaign. The degree of heroism required is the same as that required for award of a Navy Cross to an individual. The Navy Presidential Unit Citation has been in effect since October 16, 1941.

PT boats – motor torpedo boat

Q

Q boat – an armed ship disguised as a merchant or fishing ship used to decoy enemy submarines into gun range. Also called mystery ship.[31]

R

R&R – Rest and Recuperation

RAL – a type of radio receiver

Radar – radio detection and ranging. A method of detecting distant objects and determining their position, velocity, or other characteristics by analysis of very high frequency radio waves reflected from their surfaces.[32]

S

SC – a type of radio antenna

Samara – a Philippine island

Scuttlebutt – rumors or gossip (the original meaning was a fresh water keg aboard ship)

---

[31] Ibid
[32] Answers.com

Shakedown – testing a new ship or airplane under operating conditions to familiarize the crew with it and to find all the "bugs"

Shellback – one who has crossed the equator and been initiated. (A polliwog is a person who crosses the equator and is initiated by shellbacks.[33])

The Slot – a body of water about 16 to 20 miles apart from the islands near Guadalcanal; Purvis Bay.

Struck/Strike – to be in training for a particular rating

T

TAJ - a radio transmitter to keep the receivers tuned in to it

TBF – torpedo bomber plane

TBS – Talk Between Ships

Tripoli – now the capital city of Libya; formerly one of the Barbary States, which nominally were part of the Ottoman Empire; in North Africa

V

VIP – Very Important Person

V-mail - a method of microfilming U. S. forces mail to and from home to cut down on shipping costs. "V" stood for Victory

V-records – 45 RPM vinyl recordings for a record player donated by well-known recording artists such as Frank Sinatra and Bing Crosby

---

[33] Ibid

W

Walkie-talkie – a small battery-operated radio transmitting and receiving set that is usually carried on a person's back to provide two-way communication

MISCELLANEOUS

****

USS *O'BANNON* (DD450)

HAPPY HOUR[34]

Program

SKIT – RYE OR SCOTCH

Introducing MUSCOTT, Master of Ceremonies, assisted by FLEMING and POP(illegible)

DUET

We've Come a Long Way Together　　　　　　Muscott and Goff

HARMONICA SOLO

Monday
Apple Tree in the Orchard　　　　　　　　　　　　　　Hreha
White Cliffs of Dover

GUITAR SOLO

Good Luck, Old Pal
Boomer Store　　　　　　　　　　　　　　　　　　　Haynes

---

[34] Even though no liquor (booze) was allowed aboard U. S. ships, we still had some very elaborate and fun Happy Hours. This is the program from a typical Happy Hour aboard the *USS O'Bannon*.

One of the Crew, USS O'Bannon, World War II

SKIT

Fireside Chat   Guastella

SOLO

Believe Me If All Those Endearing Young Charms
Can't You Hear Me Calling, Caroline   Steil

SONGS BY THE QUINTETTE

Lamp Lighters Serenade
Moon Glow
Winter Wonderland   Quintette

GUITAR SOLO

Walking the Floor Over You
In My Dear Old Southern Home

GUITAR DUET

New River Train   Haynes & Adkison

SKIT

O'Bannon Chronicles (see below)   Steil

SONGS

A Little Foolishness   the Officers

SONGS BY THE QUINTETTE

Sweet Sue
Request Numbers   Quintette

GRAND FINALE

Shipmates Forever   Shipmates

SHIPMATES FOREVER

Shipmates stand together,
Don't give up the ship.
Fair or stormy weather,
We won't give up,
We won't give up,
The ship.

Friends and pals forever,
It's a long, long trip,
So, if you have to take a licking,
Carry on and quit your kicking,
DON'T GIVE UP THE SHIP.

One of the Crew, USS O'Bannon, World War II

CHRONICLES OF *O'BANNON*

Author Unknown (Steil?)

The words which I shall impart to you, the *Chronicles of O'Bannon*, are carved on moss-covered tablets now reposing in the inner sanctum of the Navy Department, in the Holy City of Washington, in the land of milk and honey. They deal with the travels of a ship from its promised land to the valley of the shadow and the many temptations that were placed in its way before it came to its glorious reward. Pray, sinners, pray!

In the beginning, the world was in upheaval due to the infamous treachery of the NIPPONITES, a tribe which liveth across the big pond, who steeped in sin of the first water, and with malice aforethought, had smote the followers of the faith a terrible blow and therewith laid all in chaos.

And so it came to pass that in the little fishing village of Bath, giant timbers were laid, and upon these timbers was built a mighty ark christened *O'BANNON* to sail the waters of the earth and rain down brimstone and hellfire upon the hated NIPPONESE.

And upon the ark O'BANNON was assembled many men of stout heart and limb who called themselves O'BANNONITES after their boat. Amongst these was the high priest MACDONALD, several scribes who came from high seats of learning in the east, and elders whose sole duty it was to molest the children of the ark and interrupt their hours.

And when all was in readiness, the ark did set sail on the twenty-first day of the eleventh month for waters to the south known in that day as the Caribbean, land of torrid heat. The O'BANNONITES suffered much torment, for it was hard to wear the uniform. Therein passed days and nights during which time the motley and varied O'BANNONITES passed through a stage wherein their movements were coordinated and, at last, their every action was one.

When this had come to pass and after they had defeated the Fletcher tribe in many games of skill, they returned to the land of milk and honey to prepare for the dark days ahead, to be steeped in their faith, and to gain their spare parts. And when they had come into the land, the high priests granted them three days and nights to feast and refresh themselves before embarking into the unknown.

In the ninth month, on the fourth day, the ark O'BANNON sailed for the land of the Panamanians and did visit therein many dens of iniquity. From thence, they sailed slowly many days and scarce were come over against Bora Bora; the winds suffering therein, they sailed on to the port of Noumea in the land of the New Caledonians.

And because the Chief High Priest had given the order, the ark sailed with many other vessels into the midst of the NIPPONITES.

Yea, little did the O'BANNONITES know what was in store! During the darkening night of the thirteenth day of the eleventh month, out of the nether regions came countless numbers of NIPPONESE in their own arks, which towered to the heavens. Into the midst of these sinners sailed the O'BANNONITES. And much hell was raised. From this great meeting, the hated NIPPONESE fled in great disorder, and after the O'BANNONITES had worked the enemy over with their shooting irons, they retired from the scene of destruction to a new camp one base, BUTTON by name. Herein they licked their wounds and readied themselves for fresh onslaughts with the NIPPONESE.

Thereafter followed many days and months during which the mighty ark did many tasks, many of which were to sail into the land of the NIPPONESE and did strike at their havens with thunder and lightning and did bring on them the wrath of old "67" to their complete bewilderment. The angel of mercy was riding at the foremast and the O'BANNONITES returned from these actions tired of body but pure in heart. And they thirsted for beer in order that they might perpetuate their youth. And many asked of MACDONALD, the high priest, when returneth us to the land of milk and honey, and many asked of him who sitteth at the right hand of the high priest, one PFEIFER by name, is it in faith, that which I heard?

Yea, verily, upon the tenth day of the fifth month in that year, the condition of the O'BANNONITES was "low down," and they began to bellyache amongst themselves so that MACDONALD, the high priest, took them unto the land of the Kangaroo people where they were well received, and their frustrated desires were partly fulfilled. And even as they had against the NIPPONITES, they struck gold amongst the Kangaroo people who began to murmur against the O'BANNONITES and their tribe because their wives and sweethearts were neglecting them in the daily ministration and giving out the amour to the O'BANNONITES.

And it came to pass after they had left this beautiful land that the high priest led them many times up "the slot" to rain hellfire and destruction on many "kongo class" barges belonging to the NIPPONESE, which were strongly capable of much high speed in the other direction.

On the nineteenth of the eighth month, the O'BANNONITES again proceeded up the slot with other arks, and the great birds rained thunder upon their heads from the firmament causing them to retire hastily but with their belief strengthened. And it came to pass that in the month of October, the O'BANNONITES, together with two other arks, went forth into the waters of the NIPPONITES. From the nether regions came countless enemy, numbering three for every one of the O'BANNON tribe. But the O'BANNONITES smote the NIPPONESE with the jaw bones of their 5" guns and again there was great destruction. The ark got itself rent asunder in the forward part occupied by the elders, and it was necessary to go back to the land of the ebony-skinned Espiritus, to get patched. And one GOTSCHALL, a quartermaster by trade, was straightwith called a soothsayer and prophesier since he had looked into the future and had foretold that the ark would be resting on keelblocks in the navy yard in the eleventh month of ROOSEVELT's reign.

Came the great judgment day of all! The hurts on the bow of the mighty ark had been temporarily staunched, and the word came down from above, thusly: "Lord High Priest MACDONALD, proceed ye with thy disciples, thy motley crew, to the promised land, the land of milk and honey, where shines the Golden Gate in the firmament, and there place ye into the hands of the multitudes, to commune with the faith and be reapired, and made ready for the NIPPONITE! Ye time, it has come! HALLELUJAH!" So saying, the voice spake not again, and the mighty ark headed out to the sea. It sails yet, having but a way to go, and true believers stand about the bow, waiting with outstretched hands to open with due reverence, the Golden Gate. HALLELUJAH!!

— SO SAYING, THE STORY ENDS —

One of the Crew, USS O'Bannon, World War II

Doodling aboard ship (Walter Lee)

INDEX

A. D. Chandler, 33
Action Tonight, 4
Admiralty Islands, 37
Ainsworth
    W. L. Ainsworth, 16
Aitapé, 21
Allen Summer
    USS Allen Summer, 96
Aulick
    USS Aulick, 88
Barton
    USS Barton, 96
Birmingham, 17
Bogan
    Rear Admiral Bogan, 162
Bowman, 10, 13
Boyte
    George Boyte, 14
Butler, 13, 79
Captain, Donald McDonald, 18
Cebu, 1, 137, 139, 217
Chandler, 30
Cleveland
    USS Cleveland, 84
Colorado
    USS Colorado, 84
Columbia
    USS Columbia, 84

Corregidor, 1, 3, 124, 125, 126, 127, 128, 174, 217, 218
Cutler, 13
    John Cutler, 13
Dashiell
    USS Dashiell, 96
Denver
    USS Denver, 84
Dobbin
    USS Dobbin, 151
FACTS, 2
Fathometer, 22
Fletcher, 2, 17, 27, 90, 96, 103, 106, 108, 120, 125, 129, 131, 134, 149, 174, 235
    USS Fletcher, 96
Fletcher-class, 2
Flood, 30
Florida Island Group, 16
Halsey, 27
Harry Hiller, 13
Hawaiian Islands, 1, 6, 220
Haynes
    Ensign Haynes, 17
Haynes, 41
hero of Derna, 2
Hiller, 13
    Harry Hiller, 21
Ho Islands, 2
Hollandia, 3
Honaker, 13, 79

Robert Honaker, 21
Honolulu, 17
Honshu, 160
Hopewell, 17, 174
   USS Hopewell, 55, 96
Howorth
   USS Howorth, 96
Hudson
   Joe Hudson, 79
INDEX, 239
Ingraham
   USS Ingraham, 96
James D. Horan, 4
Japanese Surrender, 2
Jenkins, 17
Laffey
   USS Laffey, 96
Lang
   USS Lang, 84
LaValette, 17
Lingayen Gulf, 1, 3, 218
Lowrey
   USS Lowrey, 96
LT(j.g.) Bonn, 78
Majuro Bay, 9
Manus Island, 37
Marine Lieutenant Presley Neville O'Bannon, 2
Maryland
   USS Maryland, 84
McDonald
   Donald McDonald, 18
Medina Plantation, 1, 33
Miller, 13, 79
Milne Bay, 19
Mindoro, 1, 3, 96, 97, 103, 104, 107, 108, 109, 110, 120, 121, 122, 123, 131, 132, 133, 136, 219, 220
Minneapolis
   USS Minneapolis, 84
Moale
   USS Moale, 96
Morotai, 3
Murphy, 10
Murray, 30
Nashville, 41, 55, 64, 90, 96, 97, 98, 99, 100, 103
   USS Nashville, 55
New Guinea Landing Operations, 1
Nicholas, 2
Noumea, 27
O'Brien
   USS O'Brien, 96
Ormoc Bay, 1, 3, 90, 92, 94, 220
Palawan, 1, 3, 97, 131, 132, 219, 220, 221
Papua, 19
Paul Hamilton
   USS Paul Hamilton, 96
PBY, 33
Pennsylvania
   USS Pennsylvania, 84
Phillip
   USS Phillip, 96
Pokomoke, 10
Portland
   USS Portland, 84
Presidential Unit Citation, 18
Pridmore
   Alfred Pridmore, 77
Pringle

USS Pringle, 96
Purvis Bay, 16
Radford, 18
Reid, 84
   USS Reid, DD369, 84
RO-115, 1
Ross, 174
Saufley
   USS Saufley, 88
Scuttlebutt, 51
Shaw
   USS Shaw, 96
Shropshire
   USS Shropshire, 55
Solomon Islands, 16
Sprague
   Rear Admiral Sprague, 71
St Louis, 17, 84
Stanley Stevens
   USS Stanley Stevens, 96
Struble
   Admiral A. D. Struble, 98

Sudet, 20
Tanahmerah Bay, 3
Tarakan, 2, 3, 147, 148, 149, 221
Taylor, 27
   USS Taylor, 55
TBS, 54
Ternate Area, 1
Thomas Timothy Murphy, 10
Tokyo Bay, 1, 2, 168, 169, 171, 173, 174, 175, 176, 177, 178, 220, 221
Treasury Island, 28
Tulagi, 16
USS *Missouri*, 2, 178
USS *Williamsburg*, 18
Walker
   USS Walker, 96
West Virginia
   USS West Virginia, 84
Wewak, 19
William D. Porter, 1, 47, 78, 144, 157, 161, 184, 185
Zamboanga, 1, 133, 134, 135, 136, 222

921 Lee, Walter Allen
LEE   One of the crew, USS O'Bannon, World War II

WITHDRAWN
Art Circle Public Library

ART CIRCLE PUBLIC LIBRARY
154 East First Street
Crossville, TN 38555-4696
1-931-484-6790

ISBN 142510917-9
9 781425 109172